ISBN 978-1-334-24354-7
PIBN 10549186

1 MONTH OF
FREE
READING

at

www.ForgottenBooks.com

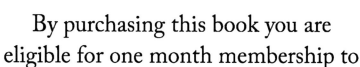

By purchasing this book you are eligible for one month membership to ForgottenBooks.com, giving you unlimited access to our entire collection of over 700,000 titles via our web site and mobile apps.

To claim your free month visit:

www.forgottenbooks.com/free549186

English
Français
Deutsche
Italiano
Español
Português

www.forgottenbooks.com

Mythology Photography **Fiction**
Fishing Christianity **Art** Cooking
Essays Buddhism Freemasonry
Medicine **Biology** Music **Ancient
Egypt** Evolution Carpentry Physics
Dance Geology **Mathematics** Fitness
Shakespeare **Folklore** Yoga Marketing
Confidence Immortality Biographies
Poetry **Psychology** Witchcraft
Electronics Chemistry History **Law**
Accounting **Philosophy** Anthropology
Alchemy Drama Quantum Mechanics
Atheism Sexual Health **Ancient History**
Entrepreneurship Languages Sport
Paleontology Needlework Islam
Metaphysics Investment Archaeology
Parenting Statistics Criminology
Motivational

BLACK'S
GUIDE TO GALWAY
AND
CONNEMARA

REVISED AND CORRECTED TO DATE BY

G. E. MITTON

SLIGO ABBEY.

BLACK'S
GUIDE TO GALWAY
CONNEMARA

AND THE

WEST OF IRELAND

Illustrated with Maps and Plans

TWENTIETH EDITION

LONDON
ADAM AND CHARLES BLACK
1912

HOTELS

The letters (I.A.C.) placed before the names of hotels indicate that such hotels have been appointed by the Irish Automobile Club, and the letter (C.) that the hotels so marked are on the Cyclists' Touring Club list.

The Editor will be glad to receive any notes or corrections from Tourists using this Guide-book. Communications to be addressed to the Publishers, 4 Soho Square, London, W.

CONTENTS

v

CONTENTS

LIST OF MAPS

ILLUSTRATIONS

GENERAL SKETCH OF THE DISTRICT.

It is not generally realised that throughout the centre of Ireland, from Sligo on the north to Limerick on the south, there runs an unparalleled fishing district, for the greater part free, consisting of a chain of lakes, almost all of which are linked together by the river Shannon. This water-way is navigable for steam launches for about a hundred miles. Salmon fishing can be had almost anywhere (except in well-known preserves such as at Killaloe), on payment of a pound a year for the licence. Trout fishing needs no licence, and the trout run large. The best centres are at Athlone, Boyle, Carrick-on-Shannon, Mount-shannon, etc. The scenery is for the greater part monotonous, level green banks and an absence of trees tending to a peaceful uniformity, but in parts of the loughs as about Mountshannon in Lough Derg, and in Loughs Key and Arrow, there is much that is attractive. What little enterprise has been attempted in the way of running public steam-boats has been chilled, and the steamers of the Upper Shannon Navigation Company now run only in the height of the summer, and traverse only the comparatively short distance from Killaloe to Banagher.

Beyond the Shannon district westward is the land of Galway, the Connemara of the tourist, with its endless opportunities for sport, and its wonderful freshness of air. Around Lough Corrib and on the intricate sea-lochs about Bertaghbhoy and Kilkieran Bays chances of sport are manifold. That land of legend and antiquities, Co. Clare, lies southward, and north-ward are Clew Bay, the Curraun Peninsula, and Achill island, all yearly attracting greater numbers of those who love scenery and wild nature.

This book deals in detail with the districts thus roughly indicated. The proper way to strike them is by starting due west from Dublin on the Midland Great Western main line which cuts Ireland in half, and the best method of reaching Dublin is, as everyone knows, by the excellent service of the London and North Western Railway. The most convenient

[The *Official A.B.C. Irish Railway Guide* (Office, Bachelor's Walk, Dublin), and *Falconer's A.B.C. Irish Guide* (53 Upper Sackville Street, Dublin); post free, 5*d.* each, are recommended.]

Page in
this book

SUMMER STEAMERS

176. **Lower Shannon** (Limerick and Kilrush, *Limerick S.S. Company, Limerick*).

Up to the last week in June, two or three times weekly, from Limerick to Kilrush (for Kilkee), and from Kilrush to Limerick.

Commencing from the last week in June, almost every weekday from Limerick to Kilrush (for Kilkee), and from Kilrush to Limerick.

The steamers stop at Kildysart, *Redgap* (Labasheeda), and *Tarbert* (for Listowel)—unless otherwise announced.

There are also frequent excursions both weekdays and Sundays. Fares to Kilrush, 6*s.* and 3*s.* 6*d.* return.

197. **Upper Shannon** (*see "Guide to Shannon Lakes," the F. W. Crossley Publishing Co., Ltd., Dublin*, 3½*d.*).—Tourist steamers now run daily from middle of June to end of September, Sundays excepted, between Banagher and Killaloe, with train connections at either end. A special day trip is run from Kingsbridge Station, Dublin, to Banagher, thence by steamer to Killaloe, and rail back to town, arriving at 10.25 P.M. Return Fares, including luncheon and tea on steamer:— 1st class, 14*s.* 6*d.*; 3rd class, 11*s.* Time is allowed for dinner at Killaloe.

209. **Galway** to **Aran Isles** (*Galway Bay Steamboat Company*, 19 *Eyre Square, Galway*) on Tues., Thur., Sat. all the year round. The service is tidal. The journey takes about three hours each way, and three hours are allowed on the islands before return. Fare, 4*s.* 6*d.* return.

213. **Galway** to **Ballyvaughan** (*see tables of above*) on Mon., Wed., Fri. during July, August, and September. Fare, 4*s.* return.

234. **Lough Corrib** (*Lough Corrib Steamboat Company, Galway*).—A steamer leaves *Galway* for Cong daily at 3 P.M. It leaves *Cong* for Galway daily at 8 A.M. The steamer stops at Kilbeg on each trip, and Annagh-down on Sats. Return Fares:—6*s.* and 3*s.* This does not allow tourists time to see Cong, but during the summer day-excursions are run, more conveniently arranged for passengers.

245. **Sligo** and **Belmullet** (*see Time Tables by Board of Works, Dublin*).— From Sligo on Tues. and Thurs.; and from Belmullet on Wed. and Fri. (May to Sept. inclusive; weekly rest of year). Excursion Fares (ret.):—7*s.* 6*d.*; 5*s.*, issued at Belmullet and Sligo (May to September inclusive). The time-table is subject to alteration.

SUMMER CARS

223. **Clifden to Westport** (Midland Great Western Railway Motor Coach, June 1 to Sept. 14, weekdays. *See Programmes of Midland Great Western Railway, Offices, Broadstone Station, Dublin*):—

		P.M.				P.M.
Clifden	*dep.*	1.30	Westport	*dep.*	1.55
Leenane	*arr.*	3.30	Leenane	*arr.*	4.45
Westport	*arr.*	6.0	Clifden	*arr.*	6.40

Light luggage only can be taken by these coaches.

train in the day from London is that leaving Euston 1.20 midday, arriving at Dublin (Westland Row) 10.20 (Irish Time). Then the "Limited Mail," the quickest train in the day leaves the M.G.W. station (Broadstones), for the west at 7 A.M., carrying a breakfast car and reaching Athlone at 9.9 A.M., and Galway 10.50 A.M. ; but for those who dislike early rising there is a choice of several other trains both from Euston and Dublin.

DUBLIN TO GALWAY.

Maynooth (*Hotel:* Leinster Arms), the seat of the well-known Roman Catholic College, is 15 m. from Dublin. The village consists chiefly of one tolerably wide street, at the end of which is the entrance to Carton, the beautiful demesne of the Duke of Leinster, open to the public on week-days ; at the other end is the ROYAL COLLEGE OF ST. PATRICK.

The college is a fine structure with two quadrangles, extended and improved in 1846 from the designs of Pugin. It has accommodation for over 500 students. The cloister is a fine specimen of Early English. The hall is a spacious and beautiful apartment, and there is a large library. The college was instituted by the Irish Parliament in 1795 to provide education for candidates for the priesthood in the Roman Catholic Church, on account of the difficulty, during the continental wars, of Irish students frequenting the foreign universities. More than half the Roman Catholic clergy of Ireland now receive their education at it. Formerly it obtained an annual parliamentary grant of £26,000 ; but at the disestablishment of the Irish Church in 1869 this was commuted by the payment of a capital sum fourteen times its amount. It is supported also by private donations and bequests, in addition to the entrance fees of the students.

The Castle of Maynooth, adjoining the college, was founded in 1176 by Maurice Fitzgerald, and repaired and strengthened in 1426 by John Fitzgerald, sixth Earl of Kildare. It was taken from Thomas Fitzgerald by Sir William Brereton, in the reign of Henry VIII., but was afterwards restored to the family. The keep and several of the towers still remain, as well as the surrounding fosse, and betoken it to have been a place of great strength.

The Protestant Episcopal Church, erected in the beginning of the 16th century by Earl Gerald Fitzgerald, has an imposing

tower. The round tower of Taghadoe is 2 miles to the north
of Maynooth.

The country soon begins to get bare and moorish. The
Wicklow hills, which relieved the flatness at first quickly disappeared, and except for the wildness of the scene, attractive
to some people, there is nothing to comment on.

A tiny branch line runs southward from *Enfield* to Eden-
derry, the source of the Boyne, which river is crossed by the
main line some miles further on.

Just before Mullingar a glimpse is caught on the south of
Lough Ennel, and with **Mullingar** itself we have reached a
famous fishing centre (*Hotels:* Greville Arms ; Brophil's). This
does not lie in the Shannon chain before referred to, but
belongs to a subsidiary set of loughs, free, and affording
excellent fishing.

A very large trade is carried on in horses, cattle, wool and
butter. The horse fair in November is attended by dealers
from all parts of Europe.

Loughs *Ennel* (or *Belvidere*), *Iron*, *Owel*, and *Derevaragh*, a
few miles from the town, give sport from April to October, and
a little further afield is Lough *Shielin*, which, on the authority
of one well qualified to judge, is " the best in the division."

Lough Ennel owes its reputation chiefly to a peculiar local method of
tricking the tackle, used during the May-fly season. This arrangement,
known as the " blow-line," suspends the whole of the gut, so that there is
no chance of the fish " getting behind the scenes."

At Mullingar the railway branches off for Sligo, subdividing
at Inny junction into another branch for Killeshandra and
Cavan, joining at the latter place the Great North of Ireland
Railway. The line to Galway bends in a south-west direction,
and as we pass from the cultivated land of the east to the
pastures of the west we note that the haunts of men are few,
the sheep many and fat. Between Castletown and *Streamstown*,
the junction for Clara, is a bare waste, and then the " dreary,
dreary moorland." At *Moate* there are two small hotels.

Athlone (pop. 7472 ; *M.G.W.* (Refreshment Room) *and G.
S. and W. Railway Stations. Hotel:* Prince of Wales) stands
on both sides of the River Shannon, which is here a fine
width, and is consequently partly in Connaught and partly in
Leinster. The river is crossed by the railway bridge (M.G.W.),

and a little lower down by the road bridge. On the Leinster or east side are the best streets, shops and the hotel, as well as the smaller station (G.S. and W). On the Connaught or west side is the principal railway station, the barracks (the town is always garrisoned), and what remains of the *Castle* now used for Military Stores. The only old part (13th century) remaining of the Castle is the base of the fort built by the Bishop of Norwich. The imposing machicolations and outer walls are modern.

The earliest fort seems to have occupied the Celtic " dun " near the present bridge, in the far-off time when the crossing was made over the fords ; and when troops and travellers knew well the hostelry and the history alike of that ancient taverner, one "Luan," to whom our best scholars trace the latter part of the name of the town. It seems strange that the place should be connected with Norwich, but it is reliable history that the Bishop of the most eastern city of England built here in 1213 the central castle of Ireland, and we shall find more of this builder-bishop's work at Clonmacnois. The castle has had an eventful record of assaults and sieges, but of none more famous than the siege of 1691, when Ginckell captured Athlone, and so forced the battle with the French and Irish at Aghrim. At first the garrison under Grace, and, later St. Ruth, who held the castle for James II., stood firm, but the heavy fire of Ginckell's men and their last assault utterly broke the Irish defence.

" It seems hard for us to conceive how, in the siege of 1691, any part of the town can have escaped utter destruction, as the batteries were all arranged along the river bank on the site of the present Strand Street, with outlying batteries. . . . But we must remember that the siege guns and powder of two hundred years ago did not carry their projectiles much farther than a couple of hundred yards. Specimens of the cannon balls used in the siege can still be seen in Athlone " (*Professor Stokes*). The present bridge replaces the old Elizabethan structure which was the scene of the siege (see *Professor Stokes's " Guide to Athlone," an uncommonly useful sixpenny-worth*).

The town owned previously two abbeys, one on each side of the river, some part of the walls (not worth visiting) remain of the Franciscan abbey on the Leinster side, near the huge tweed factories which employ so many hands that the march-past of some seven or eight hundred *boots* on the way to work at 6.30 A.M. awakes the slumbering tourist by its novelty. House accommodation is ever more and more difficult to get in this prosperous specimen of an Irish town.

The walls, built about 300 years ago, have mostly disappeared, but besides the castle fort several historic buildings remain. There is GINCKELL'S HOUSE, at the corner of Northgate Street, in which it is said the Dutchman—the famous general " who seems to have had no idea of chivalry "—lived at the time of the siege of 1691.   Of ST. MARY's CHURCH the tower with its ancient bell yet stands, from which rang out the famous " peal," referred to by Macaulay, the signal for the final assault above mentioned.

On the Connaught side of the river, once stood the abbey of St. Peter—now only remembered by its name, which survives in St. Peter's Port.

Dublin Museum has swallowed up several "finds" belonging properly to Athlone, chief among them the finest stone battle-axe in the Museum, and the gold " lunulae " (or " minn "), also from this town.

The chief feature of the town is its magnificent position in regard to the river and lakes, which gives first-rate opportunity to the angler, and makes the air of unusual freshness.   It stands just at the point where the river bursts through the range of sandhills (never rising higher than 600 or 700 feet), which runs from the Green Hills near Dublin to the shores of Galway Bay. The Prince of Wales is an old-fashioned hostelry of a comfortable sort, and stands well facing the tower of the Church, close by the gateway leading to the Deanery grounds.

Just above the town Lough Ree opens out.   A good boatman can take a passenger up the greater part of this in a day under favourable conditions.

LOUGH REE (*no steamer service*) is smaller than Derg, being 17 miles in length.   Formerly it was called Lough Ribh, and sometimes "Great Lough Allen."   The numerous promontories, bays, and creeks of the lake greatly add to the charm and variety of its scenery, and some of the islands are very beautiful ; but it all wants *sun*.

This " Lough of the Kings" formed the frontier line between Hy-Many, the principality of the O'Kelly's, on the west, and " Kilkenny West," in the kingdom of Meath, on the east.

Among several interesting islands we may mention *Inis Clothrann* (or Quaker Island), named after the sister of Queen Mab (or Meave).   On the highest point of it once stood that queen's palace, and it was on the sunny strand below that she was bathing when the cowardly Ulster chief struck her dead with a stone from his sling.   Professor Stokes states that St. Dermot is said to have lived here about the year 500 ; and the remains of seven churches can be traced.   One of these called Templemurry, is of large size ; it is said no woman could enter it and survive twelve months. The smallest Church is Templedermot, and the most remarkable, standing some distance from the others, has a square tower (the only instance in Ireland of an ancient Celtic Church thus shaped), joined or bonded on to the main building. "The monastery of *Inisbofin* (or White Cow Island) is, in some respects, the most interesting of any upon Lough Ree, because its foundation is attributed to St. Rioch, the nephew of St. Patrick, . . . a Briton or Welshman by birth." On *Hare Island* no hares are now living to explain the name; they have relinquished it in favour of the tenant, Lord Castlemaine, who has laid out the ground well. On the western shore is the interesting ruin of *Randown Castle*, "a famous spot in Irish history for the last 2000 years." In ancient times it was called John's (*Eoin*) House after a local Celtic saint; when the Normans, who hated the Celts, came and "established a castle of the Knights Hospitallers, they changed the dedication to that of St. John the Baptist." The castle still stands, with a round tower, a church dedicated to the Holy Trinity,⁣ and a fortified wall, "unique in Ireland."

Athlone is the most convenient station for visiting Lissoy, the supposed scene of Goldsmith's "Deserted Village"; and the celebrated ecclesiastical ruins of Clonmacnois on the Shannon.

Lissoy, or "Auburn," as it is sometimes called from the name in Goldsmith's poem, is 8 miles north-east from Athlone on the road to Longford, but those who are the fortunate owners of canoes will include this excursion in their visit to Lough Ree and its islands; they will find a good landing at the bay on the east shore, where the Inny flows in, about 3½ miles from Lissoy. The village is about 23 miles west·of Mullingar.

Here Goldsmith's father, the rector of Kilkenny West, added to his meagre resources by farming some 70 acres of the Lissoy Estate, but though the poet lived much of his early life here, the claim to the honour of his birthplace is disputed by Pallas, Forgney, and Elphin, which Dr. Stokes favours most. The last, indeed, has boldly asserted its right by the erection (1897) of a window in the church commemorating the event there in 1728. At Edgeworthstown (17 miles north-east) Goldsmith learnt the "Three R's," as well as the village master's long store of "stories about ghosts, banshees, and fairies." Once, alack!—on his journey between that place and his home—he "actually committed the blunder of his own Comedy, mistaking a squire's house for an inn." To enumerate, however, even the chief incidents of his life; his unhappy time at Trinity College, his idleness at home, the final departure from his native land, when he was 24 years old; to describe a career which passed from medical study to literary vagaries and philosophical vagabondism, or the distressing restraint of a moneyless author, the ill-paid production of masterpieces such as the *Vicar of Wakefield* and of the "Deserted Village," and all the events of the life of that "strange wilful scapegrace and dreamer," who afterwards became a friend of Johnson, and rose to the highest rank among the masters of the English language ; to collect all these from Forster's biography would exceed our limits. Suffice it to remind the tourist that the "Deserted Village" was published in 1770, and that he may find in the churchyard of the Temple Church in London the grave of the poet whose beautiful lines will have drawn him to this village.

It is difficult to imagine that Lissoy, even in the earlier days of Goldsmith, when he loitered on "the green" and "paused on every charm," could have so far differed from all other villages of its country as to present the distinctly English characteristics pictured in the "Deserted Village." The ruins of the "village preacher's modest mansion" are still pointed out, where the poet's father may have thought himself "passing rich on forty pounds a year." The church is said to be on the site of that "decent church" where "fools who came to scoff remain'd to pray." The same village "Mill" may perhaps be standing, and the once "glassy brook" which now, "choked with sedges, works its weary way." It is, however, scarcely probable that in Goldsmith's childhood the Inn ever offered its guests the peculiarly English comforts of the "Three Jolly Pigeons,"—

> "Where village statesmen talked with looks profound
> And news much older than their ale went round.'

The "hawthorn bush," if it ever cast its shade there, has now disappeared, owing it is said to its having been cut down piece by piece and sold to tourists. In any case, pieces of thorn now palmed off on verdant enthusiasts have not the slightest claim to be regarded as pieces of the genuine "hawthorn."

CLONMACNOIS (*Tea at Cottage. From Athlone* 8½ miles *by boat*, cost about 5s. ; 13¾ miles *by road*). The word Clonmacnois means "Retreat of the Sons of the Noble."

Far the best approach is by water, as the road curves round a long C, goes from bad to worse, and gives no sight of the ruins until you almost drop down on them. By water you get an admirable picture, the grey stone buildings, with the tall sentinel towers, standing amid green mounds, with the river lapping at their feet. On the right is the extraordinary ruin known as the Bishop's Palace (see below). The cemetery is a mass of lichened weather-beaten stones falling in every direction; and in that plot of earth, thick with the dust of countless human beings, others are still laid to rest.

What Kevin's city of Glendalough was to Wicklow, the Clonmacnois of Kieran was to the Western Irish. But, as usual, this religious settlement of the west had been established long before the saint began to build on the eastern coast. Founded about 550 by the wild winding river, Clonmacnois—"the meadow of the Sons of Nos"—stands fitly in a country where, as Dr. Petrie said, "loneliness and silence, save the sound of the elements, have an almost undisturbed reign." It occupied "in the 9th century a position second only to Armagh itself in popular reverence. . . . Two round towers, three crosses, an ancient castle, a well-preserved cashel, the ruins of seven churches, all genuine Celtic monuments, with but few traces of English work, unite to make Clonmacnois a most interesting spot for the historian or the archæologist" (*Dr. Stokes*).

The founder, St. Kieran, was "no mythical character." He was surnamed the "son of the carpenter," and after founding the church here died of "black jaundice," in 549, at the young age of 33. "In the time of Charlemagne (800) Clonmacnois was known in France and Germany as a great seat of learning, and Alcuin of York wrote . . . sending pecuniary assistance to the monks."

On entering this "Royal Cemetery," as it has been called, where—

"They laid to rest the seven Kings of Tara:
There the sons of Cairbré sleep"—

the visitor is struck by the crowd of graves and memorials of the dead. Miss Stokes has shown of what unusual value to archæologists the inscriptions found here have been in assisting them to fix reliable dates to inscriptions found in other parts of Ireland. There appear to have been twelve churches originally. and the surviving seven "all seem specimens of the true old Irish style."

Near the west wall, and outside it is O'Ruark's, or the great Round Tower, distinguished by its capless top, and a late specimen of its kind. This and the smaller one to the northeast may have been erected in the 10th or 11th century. If we accept the now most popular theory of these towers,—that, though occasionally used as emergency treasure-houses for the monasteries, they were primarily belfries,—Clonmacnois must have heard an unusual amount of bell-ringing.

Within the enclosure, near the above, is the famous **High Cross** (or "Cross of the Scriptures"), possibly the most beautiful in form and decoration of all the ancient crosses, unless perhaps the coeval "High Cross" at Monasterboice be alone excepted. From the inscriptions, which state that Colman "made this cross on the King Flann," the date has been fixed by Miss Stokes at A.D. 914. The elaborate carving represents Christ in judgment, and the building of the adjoining church by St. Kieran.

Close by is the **Cathedral** (or *Temple MacDermot*) built in 904 by King Flann Sinna and the Abbot Colman. It appears to have been rebuilt in 1089 and again in the 14th century, but the west doorway evidently survives from the earlier building. Notice the "antae" or wall-ends, so often found jutting out from the Irish west-fronts. One of the chief features is the rich north-side door, late, and carved in "perpendicular" style. St. Patrick is noticed above, between SS. Francis and Dominic (observe the quaint grin on the central face).

In the chancel, from which the once large east window has disappeared, is an inscription recording the restoration in 1647 ; on the south side is the so-called "sacristy," vaulted over with a barrel roof, and surmounted by the smallest of the three belfries. This may, perhaps, be the original oratory of St. Kieran.

A short distance from the Cathedral, on this "sacristy" side, a *Cross*, simpler and more weather-beaten than the other, stands near the west end of *Temple Hurpan*, a comparatively late church, containing within it a very early window. Not far off is *O'Melaghlin's Chapel*.

Behind the Cathedral is *Temple Kieran*, to which authorities assign the Norman date of 1167. According to the same authorities the *O'Kelly Church* close to the end of the Cathedral is coeval with it.

Near the north wall is *Temple Conor*, now the Protestant Church, where service is held once a year. *Temple Finghin* (Finan), of the late Norman period, appears to have been built into the Round Tower adjoining it, the difficulty of proving which stood here first is a nut hard in the cracking. The door of this—M'Carthy's—Tower is, like that of the High Scattery

Tower, on the ground level. "The ruins of the Episcopal *Castle* outside the cemetery of Clonmacnois are very striking ; it is still in exactly the same state as Cromwell left it 250 years ago, when his soldiers attempted in vain to blow it up. It was originally built by John de Gray, Bishop of Norwich, about the year 1210."

The gem of the whole collection, however, might very easily be missed. This is the ruin of the *nunnery* about ½ mile away. To find it follow the rough field road leading off on the east to a clump of trees, and by means of a stile enter the precincts. This little nuns' church was built in the latter half of the 12th century by Devorgil, the very flighty wife of O'Rorke, Prince of Brefny, and the cause of the English Conquest of 1172. A round-headed doorway and the chancel arch remain, and are rich in ornament, both zigzag and beaded, and are illuminated by weird suspicious faces full of witchery. The keystone of the arch has been roughly restored in order to hold it together, but wisely no attempt has been made to imitate what is inimitable.

(For detailed accounts see those by *Petrie*, and *Dr. Stokes*, *R.S.A.I. Journ.* 1890.)

Athlone is the junction for the line running north-westward to Roscommon, Claremorris, Westport, and Achill.

Ballinasloe (*Hotels :* (both I.A.C., C.) Hayden's and Imperial, 1¼ *mile from station*).—It is a dull-looking town, and unless the tourist wishes to see how its three leaden-hued streets can repose under the graceful spire of its Roman Catholic church, as indifferent about house paints as Mullingar, he should confine his visit here to the week of the GREAT FAIR.

Though annually announced for the first Tuesday in October, and the four following days, this celebrated horse and cattle fair, which has generally ranked next to the Dublin fair in importance, practically begins with, if not before, dawn on the Monday of that week, and lasts till the crush and the fun of Saturday are over. Good horses, indeed, are quickly snapped up, and the purchaser who arrives on Tuesday will find himself "out of it" by twenty-four hours.

The station, where a train of thirty or forty horse-boxes is no uncommon sight, presents a scene of overcrowding and business quite unique of its kind in Ireland. The stationmaster gives place to the barmaid of the refreshments and the lady-clerk of the telegraph; in the cloak-room beds are substituted for valises; and confusion reigns everywhere. On your right, as you enter the town, is Garbally House (Earl of Clancarty), and during the Sheep Fair the whole inner park is devoted to the use of some 20,000 bleating sheep. Within the town is bustle and bargaining. Exorbitant jarvies and excited horse-boys fill the road, or attempt, with maximum risk to life and limb, to thread their way through the groups of gaitered farmers. The latter are the most interesting figures on the street. Some, you will find, are remarkably tall, but none stout; at our last visit to the fair, the fat farmer was as much a *rara avis* as a drunken one. On the look-out for mischief is the customary cordon of police,—a painful element of Irish gatherings at present; and the dresses of the girls give colour to a crowd which, to an English eye, is as novel as it is interesting.

Five miles distant is AGHRIM, the scene of the battle (July 12, 1691) between the forces of William III. under De Ginckell and those of James II. under St. Ruth, in which the latter were completely defeated and their commander slain (St. Ruth's Bush marks the spot where he was buried). This battle is annually commemorated by the Orangemen on "The Twelfth." Twenty-two miles west of Ballinasloe is

Athenry (*Hotel:* Railway, near station), of much interest to the antiquarian, while a visit to the Dominican Friary will repay the general tourist; but the village—once a royal town— is now poverty-stricken, although still a great hunting centre, the famous "Galway Blazers" meeting here. The town was walled in 1211, and was not long in attracting foes. Its history has been a tragic one, bristling with the terrors of war. When the Earls of Clanricarde in 1577 swept the land of Connaught with fire and sword Athenry buried its full share of the slain. Again, however, it rose from its ruins, but only to fall before "Red Hugh's" destroying hand. Sacked and burnt, it never recovered from this savage blow.

Entering by the gateway in the still remaining walls you have on the left the 13th-century *Castle*, with its lofty gabled keep. In the centre of the town is the remnant of an ancient

GALWAY FAIR.

To face page IRELAND

cross in front of the gate which leads to the *Franciscan Friary*. The church, which still retains its slender tower and spire, and contains the present Protestant church within its chancel, was founded by the Earl of Kildare in 1464. The best part of the building is the south transept, which once had a very finely cut window now ruined.

A few yards off is the most interesting of all the ruins—the **Dominican Priory.** Some of the original church of 1241 still remains in the windows of the nave (south) and chancel (north), but most of it is later work. The chancel was burnt down in 1423 and, soon after, was rebuilt by the Pope's command. It has remains of an east window of the "Muckross' type ; an eccentric inscription on the north wall ; the "tasteless" tomb (in the centre) of Lady Bermingham ; and, on the south, the "sacristy," containing bones which tradition relates are those of the last monks. The nave once possessed in its west wall the finest window ("Decorated") in the church ; it had a little window in the south-west corner which is said to have lighted the cell of a penitent of the last century. The curious "coat of arms" of Tanian the smith, upon a floor slab, deserves notice. The finest feature of the building, however, is the *beautiful arcading* in the north side aisle ; if not as old as the original church, this must be at least of 13th-century date. There is an account of the church in the *R. S. A. I. Handbook*, 1897.

Athenry is on a north and south line running from Limerick to Sligo, and this belongs to the G.S. and W. Railway. We shall have to insert here the section dealing with it and those who wish to continue straight to Galway must skip to p. 206.

LIMERICK

HOTELS.—*Cruise's ;* (C.) *Glentworth ;* (C.) *George ; Hanna X.L.* (Temp.).

DISTANCES.—RAIL—Cork, 62 ; Killarney, 82 ; Tralee, 70 ; Limerick Junction, 21¾ ; Ennis, 24½ ; Kilkee, 72½ ; Galway, 98½.

    ROAD—Cork, 63¼ ; Castleisland, 52¼ ; Killarney, 64¾ ; Tralee, .63½ ; Cashel, 37¾ ; Tipperary, 25 ; Adare, 11 ; Castleconnell, 8 ; Killaloe, 14¾ ; Ennis, 21¾.

POP.—38,518.

Steamer to *Kilrush* by the Lower Shannon (*see pink pages*)

LIMERICK is not a tourist town, and its hotels are purely commercial. It is, however, a busy industrial town possessing large flour-mills, bacon-curing establishments, butter and cream factories, etc. The lace-making for which it used to be famous has been revived after a time of depression. The Shannon Fisheries Company own the important salmon fisheries, and there is scarcely any rod-fishing for strangers. As a shipping port the town ranks fourth in Ireland. It is a garrison town, and last but not least its reputation for pretty girls is amply demonstrated by facts. By adopting electric lighting, and in its fine technical schools, its Carnegie free library and public museum, the authorities show signs of care for the citizens' welfare.

Limerick is finely situated on both banks of the Shannon, at the head of the inlet known as the Lower Shannon, and is a good centre for the Lower Shannon scenery. It became the capital of the Danes, who were expelled from it by Brian Boroimhe. From 1106 until 1174, when it was conquered by the English, it was the capital of the kings of Thomond or North Munster.

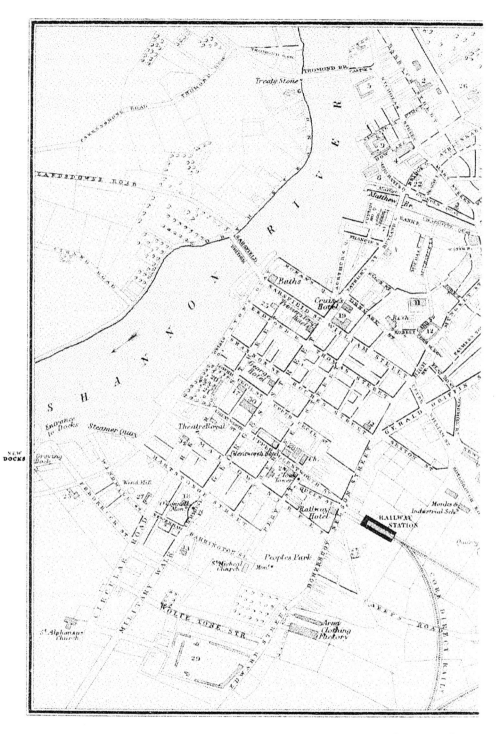

Published by A. & C. Bla

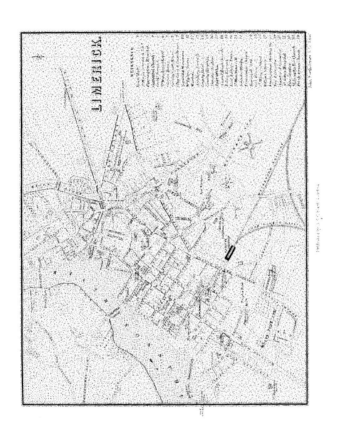

The portion on "King's island" called English Town was founded in the reign of King John by William de Burgo, who built the castle for its defence. In the 15th century its fortifications were extended to Irish Town south of it. The city in 1651 was taken by General Ireton. William III.'s siege of 1690, owing chiefly to Sarsfield's energetic defence, was raised; but 13 months later Ginckell proved too strong even for that gallant defender, and Sarsfield had to sign, upon the Treaty Stone, the famous document which bound William to respect and protect the old privileges of the Roman Catholics. The way in which the English side of the bargain was kept is sufficiently indicated by the name of *the City of the Violated Treaty*. The prosperity of the city dates from the foundation of Newtown-Pery by Mr. Sexton Pery in 1769.

BRIDGES.—English Town is connected with Newtown-Pery by New or Mathew Bridge, so named after Father Mathew (*Killarney Sect.* p. 105), and by Ball's Bridge, a modern structure occupying the site of a bridge of great antiquity. Thomond Bridge, also occupying the site of a very ancient structure connects English town with County Clare. On the Clare side of the bridge stands the "Treaty Stone" mentioned above.

By far the most impressive view of the town is that having the Treaty Stone in the foreground and looking back across the river at the walls of the castle, with the cathedral tower rising to the right.

About a quarter of a mile to the south stands Sarsfield Bridge, erected in 1831 at a cost of £85,000, connecting the County of Clare with Newton-Pery. On this bridge a statue was erected in 1855 to Lord Fitzgibbon, who fell in the charge at Balaclava. Just opposite is the Shannon Rowing Club-house, one of the prettiest and best built of its kind, a real ornament to the city. There is a long line of quays running from the Sarsfield Bridge to the floating docks, which, with the more recently constructed graving docks, have proved of great importance to the town.

Newtown-Pery.—The better streets are all situated in this part of the city, which is laid out almost with the regularity of an American city, the streets being for the most part straight, and crossing each other at right angles. *George's Street*, futilely re-named O'Connell Street by the Nationalists, contains the principal shops and warehouses, many of them of imposing

appearance. Westwards it is continued on the one side through
Richmond Place to the Military Road, and on the other along
Patrick Street through Rutland Street to New Bridge. It passes
through the west part of *Irish Town,* which is connected by the
same bridge with *English Town ;* the old gables of the houses
in both districts are noticeable. In Richmond Place there is a
statue of Daniel O'Connell erected in 1857.

In the *People's Park,* south-west of the railway station, is a
monument to Spring Rice—a lofty Ionic column surmounted by
a statue. At the junction of Glentworth Street with Upper
Baker Street there is a handsome **Clock-Tower,** erected in 1867
in honour of Alderman Tait. A statue of General Sarsfield was
erected in 1881 behind the Roman Catholic Cathedral.

King John's Castle, erected by William de Burgh in the reign
of King John for the defence of English Town, is situated at
Thomond Bridge. It is one of the most important specimens
of the old Norman fortresses now existing in the country, being
still in good preservation. Five massive towers are connected
by high walls of great thickness and solidity. On the side facing
the river the marks of shot and shell, made on the walls centuries
ago during the different sieges, are plainly visible from Thomond
Bridge. The interior of the castle is occupied by barracks, the
buildings of which, overlooking the walls, are very little in
harmony with the older structure.

St. Mary's Protestant Episcopal Cathedral, in English Town
near New Bridge, is approached through a pleasant churchyard.
On each side of the entrance path are the pinnacles of Ireton's
House (or "Galwey's Castle"), which till late in the century stood
here. It occupies the site of the palace of Donald More O'Brien,
who, about the time of the arrival of the English, 1172 A.D.,
gave up certain of his lands "in free and perpetual alms" to
Brictius, then Bishop of Limerick. The diocese of Limerick
dates, however, from the 5th century, but the primitive cathedral,
which occupied the site of the present St. Munchin's Church,
was destroyed in the 9th century.

The cathedral, rebuilt on the new site about 1180, was
enlarged in 1207 by the addition of a chancel. It subsequently
underwent alterations of various kinds. It was restored in 1860.

Parts of the fine *West Door* are ancient, and the modern work
is good. The *tower* has a modern top surmounted by the
"stepped" pinnacles and battlements of the Jerpoint character

(*Killarney Sect.* p. 137).   Battlemented parapets of the same kind run round the nave and chancel.

Within is sombre gloom.   There is little architectural ornament besides the scraps of Norman mouldings and shafts spared by a pitiless stucco-brush, and a fine bit of *arcading* in the **S. Transept.**   In the latter transept is the Galwey tomb ; and the tracery of the near window of the adjoining **South Aisle** should be observed.   It is a network of interwoven "ogees" of uncommon design.

The remarkable *misericorde seats* of carved oak in the nave are well worthy of notice.   The old oak carving is a rare thing in Ireland, and here this woodwork, probably cut about 1490, is "the most curious feature of the church" (*R.S.A.I. Journal,* 1895).

The arcading just outside the churchyard, and now in ruins, is a remnant of the *Old Exchange* which was taken down with Ireton's House some years ago.

The bells are eight in number and in the key of F.   The oldest, the D and F bells, bear Latin inscriptions with the date 1673.   During the siege of the city in 1690 a cannon was mounted by the Irish on the battlements of the cathedral, from which a shot, directed by a very skilful gunner of the name of Burke, nearly proved fatal to King William.

St. John's Roman Catholic Cathedral is reached from St. Mary's Cathedral by Mary and John Streets.   It is adorned by one of the handsomest spires in Ireland, and, within, by a dark and elaborate stone *reredos* over the great altar.   Between the south altars is a very beautiful marble **statue by Benzoni** of the Virgin Mary—perhaps *the* work of art in Limerick.

The best of the other churches is that of the *Redemptorists*, a short walk southwards along George's Street and Military Road. This large building contains in the north aisle a bronze statue of St. Peter (?), with toes polished to an unusual extent by a curious means.

The best **excursions** are to Adare; the Lower Shannon (*steamer*); Castleconnell ; Killaloe, Lough Derg and the Upper Shannon (*steamer*).   For distances see p. 188.

EXCURSION TO ADARE.

This is an enjoyable trip and deserves a day of good sunny
weather. It may be accomplished either by rail or road, the
two running very close together. In ¾ mile join the cross
roads (right) and then forward again. At *Patrickswell*, 5½ miles
is a *Well* (right) with fragmentary carving, said to have been
broken by a soldier's bullet.

Adare Manor is the seat of the Earl of Dunraven. In the
demesne is one of the most remarkable assemblages of ruins in
the kingdom. The word Adare, in old documents *Athdara*, the
Ford of the Oak, sufficiently indicates the character of the trees
which once lined the banks of the Maigue.

Adare (*Hotel* : (I.A.C.) Dunraven Arms). — The hotel is
under the estate management and is good. Much frequented
in the hunting season by sportsmen who hunt with the Co.
Limerick hounds. Tickets (free) for the house and ruins to be
had on application at estate office in the village.

The history of Adare goes back to the erection of the Rath, the early fort
on which the castle of the Normans was built about the twelfth century.
Around this and the church, also built then by the invaders, grew the
Norman town which was populous enough in 1226 to obtain the English
king's grant for an annual fair. Then large religious houses were established,
and the town enclosed within walls, which have now practically disappeared.
"At the commencement of the present century Adare had dwindled down
to a collection of thatched cottages," numbering less than two dozen (*Dunraven Memorials*); but with the coming of the second Earl of Dunraven
(1824–1850), fortune smiled upon it again.

The Village Gate of **Adare Manor** is opposite the hotel. For
a view of the *House* turn right when the path forks within.
It is a fine modern mansion built in 1832, and "the greater
portion" was "designed by an amateur, a mason named
Conolly, . . . not a single drawing having been furnished by
an architect" (*Memorials*). The special feature to note is the
beautiful modern oak carving on overmantels, staircase, etc., all
done by local talent.

The Quin family is from the younger branch of the descendants of Olioll
Olum, King of Munster in the 3rd century.

The left road from the above fork leads to the *Poor or* **Franciscan** Abbey, said to be the most celebrated of all the Munster monasteries. The foundation stone was laid in 1464, but most of the arches and much of the work are rude and plain. The effective tracery of the south and east *windows* is similar to that at the Augustinian Abbey, and at Muckross, Killarney. One is reminded of the latter ruin also by the **cloisters** on the N. side, much darkened by a giant central yew-tree.

Across the grass, and near the village bridge, are seen the remains of the **Castle**, also within the park. A castle is known to have stood here before 1226, and may have been founded some years previously by the Anglo-Normans. "On the attainder of 'silken' Thomas, in 1536, the castle was forfeited to the Crown," and, passing to the Desmonds, was called *Desmond Castle*. It was dismantled by Cromwell. The Gate Tower contains the groove for the portcullis. Of the keep, built on the ancient *Rath*, the ruins are not imposing; they are south-east of the inner ward. Near the castle is the old *Parish Church* of St. Nicholas. The chancel contains probably the original Norman walls, is "about the oldest building now remaining in Adare," and dates from something between 1280 and 1320. In 1806 it ceased to be used for the Protestant service, which was transferred to the Augustinian building.

On the left (or west) as you come out of the Village Gate is the **White Abbey** of the Trinitarians, which was founded before 1299. The Church, which is now the *R.C. Church*, was at the beginning of the century a ball-alley, and but for the good (second) Earl would have become a potato store. Its chief feature is the massive central tower. The spacious and good interior is beautified by the reredos screen.

The adjoining *Fountain* was the gift of the (second) Countess, 1851.

Close to the Bridge, and nearer Limerick, is the **Black Abbey** of the Augustinians, founded in 1315 ; part of which is used as the Protestant Church. The slender proportions of the tower, as of that of the Franciscan Abbey, will strike the visitor, as well as the "Muckross" tracery of the east window of the Church. This was restored in 1852, but the interior is still choked up, not only by the heavy tower supports, but by the Dunraven pews. The later *cloisters* have a lavatory sink ; the *Refectory* is now the school.

13

FROM LIMERICK DOWN THE SHANNON.

By steamer on the Shannon to Kilrush, thence by train to Kilkee.
A bill of sailing, with fares, should be obtained from Lower Shannon
Office, Limerick, or Kilrush.

Shortly after leaving the quay at Limerick we pass on the left,
or County Limerick side the beautiful demesne of Lord Emly, at
the extremity of whose property the rocky eminence of Carrig-o'-
Gunnel (Rock of Connel), crowned by the picturesque ruins of an
ancient castle, forms a prominent object of the landscape. The
castle, originally founded by the Knights Templar, was blown up
and dismantled after its surrender to the forces of William III.
in 1691.

On the Clare side, nearly opposite Lord Emly's demesne, are
the extensive woods of Cratloekeel, covering the mountain's side.
Farther on we pass Dromore Castle, the magnificent residence of
Lord Limerick, and Beagh Castle, and Horse Rock Lighthouse,
the latter a prominent object in the middle of the river. On the
Clare side (right), before reaching Foynes, we pass the estuary of
the Fergus, called Lough Fergus. This is a very archipelago ;
and on Canon Island is an ancient Norman monastery. Behind
Beeves Lighthouse (left), in mid-stream, is the mouth of the Deel
river, on which is—

ASKEATON (railway station), remarkable for its ancient buildings. Its Norman
castle of the Desmonds ; Knights Templars' Church ; and Franciscan Abbey
(1419), with uncommon cloisters, are all worth visiting.

Four miles inland, and south from Askeaton, is Ballingrane Junction,
which is 2 miles from *Rathkeale* station. Here is another Desmond Castle
and several ancient buildings, including an "Early English" Priory. At
the beginning of the last century some Lutheran refugees from the Palatinate
settled in this neighbourhood.

Then, leaving the disused pier of Foynes on our left, we put
in on certain days in the week at **Kildysart**, which serves the
wide trainless district between Ennis and Kilrush. On other
days the steamer continues until **Redgap**, on Labasheeda Bay,
is reached. A little beyond, and on the opposite side of the
Shannon, is the bright, well-built village of **Glin.**

Glin Castle has been for centuries the seat of the Knight of Glin, called
the "Red Knight," to distinguish this branch of the Fitzgerald family from
those of the White Knight, and the Black Knight (of Kerry).

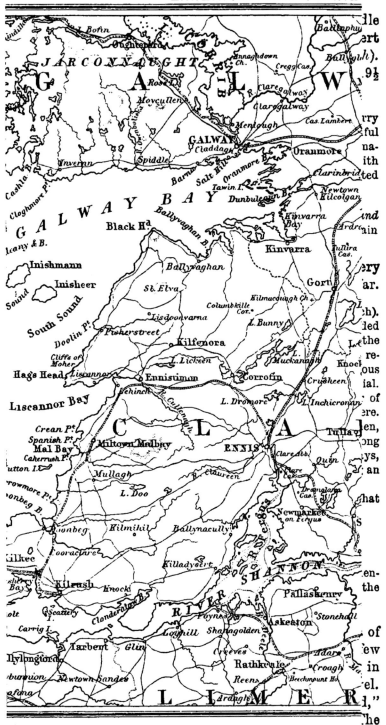

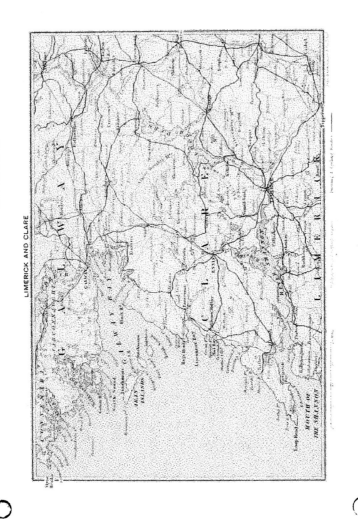

About 5 miles from Redgap, along this well-named "idle river," are the tall lighthouse and crumbling pier of **Tarbert** (*Hotel*) ; Listowel Railway station is 12½ miles away (*Coach*). From *Listowel* it is by rail 50¾ miles to Limerick ; to Tralee, 19½ miles ; and 9½ miles to Ballybunnion.

Ballybunnion (*Castle Hotel*), on the south of the Shannon, on the Kerry coast, is a favourite seaside resort, and has many attractions—a beautiful beach, high cliffs with caves and natural rock-arches of wondrous forma-tion, and most interesting walks in all directions. It is connected with Listowel by a "Lartigue" railway, the first constructed in the United Kingdom. The rail is a single one, raised 3 feet from the ground.

A special Government (Balfour) boat plies locally between *Tarbert and Kilrush*, thus connecting the south-side coach with the north-side train service, but only in the season.

Soon after leaving Tarbert the round tower of **Scattery Island** comes into view, and beyond it Loop Head, dim and far.

The older name of Scattery is *Inis* (the island) *Cathaig* (of the Cathach). The latter was a monster, mastered and chained by St. Senan, who founded in the 6th century cells and oratories in County Cork, the islands of the Fergus, on Mutton Island, and upon this island. He died in 544, and is re-vered as patron in several French churches. The monastery became famous and attracted Kieran, founder of Clonmacnoise, who became an official. Even St. Aidan, "founder of Lindisfarne, and consequently predecessor of the Bishops of Durham," *may perhaps* have been the Aidan who lived here. We read of the house being destroyed twice in the 9th century by Norsemen, devastated by Brian Boru, plundered by the Danes, and captured and long held by the English. Granted as a fishing village to Limerick in later days, it passed to the mayor of that city, who "asserted his rights by shooting an arrow into the river west of the island" (*Killarney Sect.* p. 115).

The legend of St. Cannara, which Moore has put into verse, tells how that holy nun sailed to Senan's island to make her request—

> I come with humble heart to share
> Thy morning and thy evening prayer.

But the good lady met with as stern a refusal as the gentle Kathleen of Glen-dalough, and being a relative of St. Senan was allowed only to receive the Blessed Eucharist, and, after death, was buried on the foreshore.

There is an interesting description of the ruined buildings of Scattery in the *R.S.A.I. Handbook*, 1898 (*Westropp*) ; a few notes will here suffice. The **Round Tower** is the tallest in Ireland, and is exceptional in having a door on the ground level. Miss Stokes notes that as its masonry is not "hammer-dressed," it may be dated among the earliest (9th to 10th century). The

Cathedral, between the tower and the shore, is of the same date; it has a good specimen of the early west doors. The *Clogh Oir*, or "Golden Bell" of Senan is still preserved by the Keane family of Ennis, hereditary keeper ("coarb") of the treasure, and Miss Stokes believes it to be "the very bell used by the founder." On the north side of the cathedral is an **Oratory** of large and early masonry, with a romanesque chancel arch of later date. West of the tower is the **Well** (or "tober") of Senan; and **Temple Senan** is a chapel, much rebuilt, on high ground, some 170 yards away to the north. Tradition says that **Ard-na-n-Angeal**, 300 yards south-west of tower, is the height on which the saint communed with the angel before defeating the "cathach." There are also ruins of the later **Temple-a-Marv** (of the dead), and a 16th-century **Castle**.

Kilrush (*Hotel:* Vandeleur Arms) is our last pier. From this small market town it is 8½ miles by train to Kilkee; and for the journey a special train (not always published) awaits the arrival of steamers. Change at Moyasta Junction.

Kilkee (*Hotels:* Moore's; Falvy's Royal Marine; West End (season only); Stella Maris; Victoria) is one of the most charming watering-places in Ireland, finely situated in the neighbourhood of a great variety of magnificent rock scenery. The bay is sheltered from the waves of the Atlantic by a ledge of the Dunganna rocks. The town is built close to the sea, along a semicircular strand with a bright, smooth sandy surface. Baths have been erected near the beach, and there are also chalybeate springs. Irish moss is found in great quantities in the neighbourhood, and the sea-pinks grow in profusion. There is good bathing in the bay, and every second house has apartments to let. Kilkee has reached the stage of being comfortable without being too sophisticated, and may be warmly recommended. Mixed bathing allowed round the corner! There are good golf-links.

Puffing Hole, Look-out Cliff, the *Amphitheatre,* and *Bishop's Island* are all bits of this remarkable coast that should be seen.

The latter has an early oratory; and legend places here a bishop, who fled from the famine-stricken mainland to feast on his private island store. When, however, the famine and his own fare were alike at an end, and this fasting philanthropist sought to return, the raging sea had widened the chasm and chained him to his solitary fate. In the bay, behind, the

Intrinsic perished in 1835, amid scenes of great distress. Above the sinking ship and drowning women a seagull was seen to hover; and soon after the same bird turned shoreward and dropped among the people on the cliff a lady's glove.

The **Cave of Kilkee** is about 2 miles from the town, and is best visited by boat from the harbour, a fine view being in this way obtained of the cliff scenery along the shore. The arched entrance to the cave is about 60 feet in height. Our attention is at once attracted by the numerous jutting rocks, the stalactites depending from the roof, and the "variety of rich metallic tinges from the copper, iron, and other mineral substances held in solution by the water." As we proceed into the cave it gradually diminishes in height.

The walks along the coast are of great interest, especially southwards. The dark rocks of chipping flakes, hollowed beneath and broken into fantastic shapes by the waves, form a grand setting to the luminous blues, greens, and snowy foam of the Atlantic breakers.

Loop Head (16 *miles from Kilkee*), properly Leap Head, or Cuchullin's Leap. The tradition is that Cuchullin a knight of Ulster, on being pursued by a termagant woman called *Mal*, reached the extremity of Clare, and discovering that she was still close in pursuit, leapt on to a small rock about 25 feet from the mainland. The termagant succeeded also in reaching the rock, whereupon Cuchullin immediately leapt back, but the woman, not succeeding in her second attempt to follow him, fell into the waves and perished.

See West Clare Railway, pp. 204, 214.

CASTLECONNELL AND THE FALLS OF DOONAS.

From Limerick these may be reached either by rail (about 9¾ miles) or road (Falls, 6 miles; Castleconnell, 8 miles). The railway line is that going to Killaloe by way of Killonan. Visitors who choose this method will have to cross Castleconnell Bridge, and walk back about a mile or more along the river bank to the Falls. By road either side of the river may be taken, but the most usual way is to go by the west side and return by the east, visiting Castleconnell *en route.* Cyclists following this method are advised to keep to the main road until they reach Cloonlara Church, as though there are several tempting roads leading off on the right, they turn and twist so much that no distance is saved, and the cyclist may find himself well on the way back to Limerick without intending it. From Cloonlara turn right, and continue straight down to the river side by a gate opening on to the well-kept lawn of the Angler's Rest, a charming little tea-house of a kind unusual in Ireland. Visitors are received here for a night in a simple way and anglers often stay for weeks. From here the path to Castleconnell may be followed along the river's bank, but this necessitates the negotiation of several awkward gates, and cannot be commended to cyclists. This walk runs through the grounds of Doonas House, the ancient seat of the family of Lord Massy, whose residence, Hermitage, is on the other side of the river, not far from Mountshannon, which extends for more than a mile beside the water. On this side, the east, there is a path near Hermitage which also gives a view of the Falls. At the end of the walk through the grounds of Doonas there is a ferry to Castleconnell.

The **Falls or Rapids of Doonas** have no sudden drop, but extend over a slope of a mile or more of broken water diversified by moss-covered boulders. In flood-time not a stone is to be seen, nothing but the boiling, angry water. The great breadth of the river, and the innumerable rocky islets, some bare and dark, others having stunted trees or shrubs, give much variety to the scene.

Castleconnell (*Hotels:* (C.) The Shannon ; Castle (small)), 9¾ miles from Limerick by rail and 8 miles by road, is finely situated on the Shannon. In the vicinity of the village there is a chalybeate spring, at one time much frequented.

The village, much cleaner and neater than most Irish villages, takes its name from an old castle of the O'Briens, kings of Munster, which crowns a high and solitary rock overlooking the Falls of Doonas. The grandson of Brian Boroimhe is said to have been inveigled into the castle by the Prince of Thomond, who, having put out his eyes, afterwards cruelly murdered him. The fortress was subsequently occupied by Richard de Burgo, the Red Earl of Ulster. In 1688 it held out for King James, but was taken after a siege of two days, and blown up with gunpowder.

Though Castleconnell is to be ranked high upon the fisherman's list, there is hardly any free fishing, and the salmon fishing is let at the usual rates. The hotel is in the hands of the firm, *Knight and Son*, after whom the well-known rods are called. Two 46 lb. salmon were in the list of those caught here in the season.

O'BRIEN'S BRIDGE crosses the Shannon a few miles above Castleconnell. In 1537 Conor O'Brien, King of Thomond, had aided "Silken Thomas" in his rebellion against Henry VIII. The king determined to subdue Conor, and ordered the Lord Deputy, Lord Leonard Gray, to compel him to renounce the Papal supremacy and swear allegiance to the English king. Conor not only did so, but promised to help the English in breaking the bridge. The present structure, however, bears such a venerable aspect that we might almost believe it to be the identical O'Brien's Bridge.

Killaloo (*Hotels:* (I.A.C., C.) Lakeside; (C.) Grace's; (C.) Royal; Shannon View), by rail 17¼ miles from Limerick, and at the south end of Lough Derg, is a very ancient town.

It is a difficult place to describe as it is so peculiar, with its high green banks, its colour-washed clean houses, the tower of the cathedral, its old grey stone bridge with the salmon-weir above and the eel weirs and tanks below. It is the paradise of the angler who doesn't mind paying a reasonable price for good sport. The fishing is all preserved with the exception of a strip on the east bank in February and March, and a boat and boatman cost 10s. a day. The season lasts from February to October, inclusive. The Lakeside Hotel is very large, standing in its own grounds, with fine views, near the steamer quay behind the station. The other three hotels are grouped near the end of the bridge on the opposite shore. Grace's, though small, is exclusive, with an aristocratic clientèle, and is more or less private, having no bar. It has stretches of rod-fishing to let, as have some of the other hotels, but as these vary from year to year, enquiries are best made on the spot.

The first church was founded here in the 6th century by St. Dalua, who gave his name to the place, and was succeeded by Flannan in this bishopric. The *oldest church* in the town is the little chapel close to the cathedral, with a very high-pitched roof; this "Petrie considers . . . to be attributed to St. Flannan" (*Murray*). The massive tower of the Norman **Cathedral** is that building's most striking feature; the upper brown part with battlements is much later than the gray portion beneath. There is a very elaborate *Norman Door*

inside the church (south wall), which may perhaps have led
to King O'Brien's tomb.

"Kinkora," the palace of King Brian Boru, once stood, so
says the story, near the bridge of Killaloe.

Lough Derg or **Dearg** is the largest lake in the course of the
Shannon, being 23 miles in length. The Shannon *steamer*
leaves Killaloe early in the morning, and after traversing the
whole length of the Lough, goes on up the Shannon to Banagher.
This is only in the season. See *pink pages.*

Though the southern entrance, as also indeed the northern
end of the lough, has no attractions comparable with the central
reaches, the boat passes very pleasantly between the green
quarried slopes of Arra Mountain on the right and the Slieve
Bernagh on the left.

There is certain soft beauty about *Scariff Bay* (*pier*). On
its north side is **Iniscaltra** ("the island burying-ground"), or
Holy Island on which are some ancient buildings of unusual
interest. St. Caimin founded a church here in the 7th century,
and in all probability the western end of the *church* now standing is part of that building. The chancel, however, is much
later, and is dated by Miss Stokes 1007 A.D. It was, she says,
"built by King Brian Borumhe (Boru), and this building marks
the transition to the enriched round-arch style of Ireland."
It is thus an important basis for dating many ancient buildings
in Ireland. From the remnants remaining, it is evident that
the west door was richly carved. Hard by is a *Round Tower* of,
perhaps, the 10th century, which is all of one kind of stone, and
shows the "first idea of the arch." The chronicler Marian
"speaks of a St. Anmchadh, who, coming from Iniscaltra,
travelled to Germany, and became a recluse at Fulda" (*Stokes*).

On the same side as Scariff Bay is *Mountshannon*, where
there is a comfortable old-fashioned hotel which can put up 20
to 30 anglers in the season. "Dapping" with the natural
fly is a favourite method of the sport in early summer. The
charge per day for man and boat is 7s. 6d. Otherwise fishing
free. The Shannon steamers do not stop here but at *Williamstown*, a short distance above. The scenery around Mountshannon is pretty enough to satisfy those who have no taste for
fishing. On the opposite side of the lough is *Youghal Bay*,
across which we have a good view of the Devil's Bit Mountain,

KILLALOE.

W. Lawrence, Dublin.

so called from the curious notch in its outline. According to
the tradition it was the devil who bit the piece out of the
mountain, but, finding the morsel too hard for his digestion,
he is said to have vomited it at Cashel in Tipperary, where it
is known as the "Rock of Cashel." The pier in Dromineer
Bay (*Hotel*), the next inlet on this east shore, serves the town of
Nenagh, 6 miles inland, and faces the charming house called *St.
David's.*

Between this and *Island More* we get the best scenery on
the loch, and obtain a good view of the well-defined and
highest point in Silvermine Mountains to the south, beyond
Nenagh. Away to the west, behind Williamstown, are the
Scalp and other points of the Slieve Aughty group, dim
and far.

Then the "Devil's Bit" pops up again on the right, behind
the ruined tower of Castle Biggs, and on the left (west) we pass
Rossmore (*pier*) before seeing the Clanricarde Castle and
demesne on the same side. The principal shooting preserves
here are owned by Lord Clanricarde and the Earl of Westmeath.

Portumna (*Inn*) is in a somewhat decayed condition, and
possesses the ruins of a monastery and the remains of an ancient
castle. The monastery, which belonged to the Dominican friars,
was founded on the site of a very ancient Cistercian chapel dedicated to St. Peter and St. Paul. The Dominicans were confirmed
in their possession by a bull of Pope Martin V. dated 8th October
1426. The walls are comparatively entire. The council, presided
over by the Earl of Strafford, convened for the purpose of estab-
lishing His Majesty's claim to the forfeited estates in Connaught,
held its sitting in Portumna Castle, but the members having
refused to admit the royal claims were sent to Dublin as prisoners
under escort of the sheriff.

A brief view of the "Abandoned Railway" may be had on
the east (right) bank just after leaving Portumna Bridge. The
end of the deep cutting is visible for a moment. This twelve-
mile line was laid down between Portumna and Parsonstown,
but owing to a dispute between the Company and the Board of
Works it was abandoned. The country-folk ripped up the rails
and sleepers. A motor bus runs twice a day each way between
Portumna and Ballyquirk.

We have now fairly left Lough Derg, and are once more sailing against the placid stream of the river through a country that is "sometimes tame, sometimes ugly, not seldom beautiful, but never either grand or picturesque." On each side are flat meadows supplying good grazing, and dropping to the river in a fringe of rushes which provides many a snuggery; for the extensive population of waterfowl. The chief features on the landscape are the red and black guide-posts, which are, doubtless, indispensable to "the man at the wheel" in flood time.

A few miles above Portumna the Shannon was almost unnavigable until the commissioners deepened the bed of the river. During these operations a number of very interesting prehistoric relics were brought to light. In the greatest depths stone hatchets were found. In a stratum overlying this were bronze spears and swords ; a still nearer deposit contained implements of iron, such as swords and spear-heads ; and in the strata next the surface more modern implements, among which were antiquated firelocks.

Banagher (*Hotels :* M'Intyre's ; (C.) Miss Miller's (Temp.)) is a market town on the left bank of the river, and the railway terminus of a branch line from Clara. The river is here crossed by a fine stone bridge of seven arches, completed in 1843, which is protected by two towers and a battery : connected with it there are large barracks. About a mile from the town is the well-known Banagher distillery. In the vicinity are the ruins of Garry Castle, the ancient fortress of the Macloghlans, the last representative of whom died a little more than half a century ago. He has been regarded as the "last Irish chief."

At Banagher those who have come by rail from Dublin meet the Shannon steamer to go south. Northward the river winds away 32 miles to Athlone, 8½ miles short of which are the celebrated ruins at Clonmacnois (see p. 182) but there is no means of traversing this part of the Shannon except by private enterprise.

LIMERICK TO SLIGO BY RAIL via ENNIS, ATHENRY AND TUAM JUNCTION.

After "fetching a compass" round the entire eastern half of the city, the line crosses the low-banked Shannon ; and from the bridge we get far and away the best view of Limerick, in which the beautiful spire of the R.C. Cathedral is the leading feature. Then running over well-wooded flats we pass Cratloe Castle, and Bunratty Castle, once the seat of the De Clares and the Thomonds, with histories which moved Thackeray to romance wildly over two pages of his *Sketch Book.*

Beyond Six-mile Bridge the rails pass between some small lakes (right) and—3 miles to the left—*Newmarket-on-Fergus*. This village is just south of Dromoland, the seat of Lord Inchiquin, which is in sight from the train (left). The family (O'Brien) claim descent from King "Brian Boru," who fell at Clontarf, 1014.

About 2 miles up-stream from *Ardsollus Station* (19¾ miles) is QUIN ABBEY, an extensive and well-preserved ruin, founded for Franciscan friars, and dating probably from 1402. An examination of the ruins would seem to indicate that the building had been added to at different periods. It has recently been restored at great cost. It is of special interest as having been surrounded by a fortress, either of Norman period or earlier. In the adjoining cemetery there are some ancient monuments. The best things at **Clare Castle** (23 miles) are the fine meadows, with the ruins of a castle situated on a small island in the river Fergus. Close to the railway line (right) are the fine ruins of Clare Abbey, founded in 1195 by Donald O'Brien, King of Munster, for Augustinian canons regular.

Ennis, 24½ miles (Ref.-Rm. ; *Hotels:* (C.) Old Ground ; (I.A.C., C.) Queen's ; (I.A.C.) Carmody's), is one of the most cheerful-looking towns in Ireland, and, whilst comparing well in this respect with Sligo, wears more signs of prosperity than Cork, Waterford, and several other towns of greater fame. It is clean and has good houses, buildings, and some fair shops. The people are of unusually brisk and business-like character. On the far side of O'Connell's cloud-swept statue is the chief historical building—the *Franciscan Abbey.* The chancel arch of this 13th-century building supports an unpleasant but curious tower bristling with late and spiky pinnacles. The pleasantest bit of the town, as usual, is at the *Bridge* over the brown and rushing river which gives the place its name. Beyond the Infirmary is the "*Martyrs'*" *Pillar*, erected in memory of the trio "who suffered death in Manchester, 1867"; and chiefly noticeable for the inscribed details concerning its builders, even to the name of the stone-

cutter. In the R.C. Cathedral is an unusually realistic and
coloured group of figures before the N. altar. Some mural
paintings should be observed.

From Ennis the *West Clare Railway* passes westward by Corofin, where
there is good fishing in Lough Inchiquin, Ennistymon (station for Lisdoonvarna), Lehinch, Miltown Malbay, Kilkee (47 miles), and Kilrush on the
Shannon. See page 214.

Beyond Ennis limestone in fragments appears to be the
despair of the farmer, for even the innumerable miles of inter-
secting walls do not exhaust so fertile a crop. Soon after you
see Inchicronan Lough, which encircles the island ruin of
O'Brien's 12-century abbey. *Tubber* ("the well") is one mile
over the Galway county boundary ; and a few minutes after
passing Loughcutra Castle, you see the conspicuous spires and
the prettily embowered school of

Gort (32¾ miles), a comparatively prosperous town, with a
barracks, workhouse, etc.[1] The town takes its name from the
time when King Gnairt had a palace there. Three miles south-
west of Gort is Kilmacduagh, with 7th-century ruins, an
ancient fort, and a round tower which leans considerably from
the perpendicular.

At *Athenry Junction*, 60¾ miles (see page 187) we cross the
Midland Great Western Railway for Galway.

From Athenry it is 16 miles northwards to **Tuam** (*Hotel :*
Guy's Imperial), a pleasant, and in some ways smart little
town. On the other hand it looks the humblest of *cities ;* yet
it remained the seat of a Protestant archbishop as late as 1834,
and traces its importance back to the 6th-century saint Jarlath,
who founded a monastery here. There are some good houses
and one or two large shops. In the centre is a fine ancient **Cross**
with carvings, described thus by Miss Stokes :—" Crucifixion
on one side ; figure of a bishop on the other ; a funeral procession, apparently, on the reverse." There are inscriptions
both ancient and modern, and much interlaced work.

The chief buildings in the town are the two Cathedrals, that of St. Mary
(Church of Ireland) and that of St. Jarlath (Roman Catholic). The former
carries the mind back to the time when Ireland was divided into a number
of small kingdoms, and when Tuam was the metropolitan see for Connaught.
At that time there were seven churches in Tuam. Of these ancient churches

---

[1] " It looked as if it wondered how the deuce it got into the midst of such
desolate country, and seemed to *bore* itself there considerably."—Thackeray.

nothing remains but the chancel of St. Mary's and a small part of the old parish church, which now stands in the middle of the ancient burial ground close to the present Cathedral. The chancel arch is of Hiberno-Romanesque architecture, and consists of six circumscribed semicircles, elaborately ornamented in low relief. Dr. Petrie, in writing of the church, says, "Of the ancient church of Tuam the chancel only remains; but fortunately it is sufficient to make us acquainted with its general style of architecture, and to show that it was not only a larger, but more splendid structure than Cormac's church at Cashel, and not unworthy of the powerful monarch to whom it chiefly owed its erection. The arch mouldings consist of diamond, fret, and varieties of the chevron, all carved with exquisite perfection. The original East window of the chancel remains. It is a triplet carved with most elaborate interlaced work, like that of the ancient Irish crosses. This window is one of the most perfect examples I know of interlaced ornament in stone." Joined to the East end of the Cathedral is a much older church, which was used as a Cathedral till the present one was opened in 1878, after being fifteen years in erection, at an outlay of over £20,000. The old church is now used as a Synod Hall, a portion of it being set apart as a Diocesan Library. This valuable library was presented to the diocese by the Rev. Jos. Henry, D.D., formerly British chaplain in Lima, Peru. In the Synod Hall are some beautifully carved and inlaid choir stalls, which were found in Italy and were purchased by the late Mr. E. J. Cooper of Markree Castle, for £3000, and after his decease presented to the diocese.

Outside the *Roman Catholic Cathedral*, at the far end of the town, are several statues, including one to Father MacHale, by Farrell. Within is a *baldachino* of marble.

After Tuam we go on to **Claremorris**, a junction with the Midland Great Western line to Westport, and from thence there is nothing to remark on till **Collooney**, 7 miles south of Sligo, where we join the rails of the other company to run into the terminus, see p. 246.

Collooney has come into prominence in connection with the railway to Belmullet planned to form a link in the "All-Red Route" between Great Britain, Canada, and Australia. The new line is 90 miles long, and the terminus is to be at Blacksod Bay. By this method it is reckoned that 24 hours can be saved on the journey. Belmullet Harbour is one of the finest in Ireland, and the new harbour works will adapt it to receive a line of ocean steamers.

Having thus completed the tour of the cross-line between Limerick and Sligo, we may resume our journey westward from where we left it off at Atheury (p. 187) en route for Galway.

GALWAY.

HOTELS.—(I.A.C., C.) *Railway* at the Station; *Mack's Royal*; and others smaller in Eyre Square; *Eglinton*, Salthill.

DISTANCE from Dublin 126¼ miles. Galway to Spiddle by car (11½); by rail to Clifden, *viâ* Oughterard (46).

STEAMERS.—To and from Ballyvaughan three times a week in summer; every second day all the year to the Aran Islands.

CHIEF PLACES OF INTEREST.—Protestant Church of St. Nicholas; Lynch Castle and other specimens of ancient street architecture; University College; Claddagh; Salthill; Bay of Galway; Islands of Aran.

POP. 13,255.

Almost nothing is known of the history of Galway until the arrival of the English, when the town and adjoining district were under the protection of O'Flaherty. In the 13th century it was given to Rich. de Burgo, who strengthened its fortifications and made it the residence of a number of enterprising settlers, the principal families of whom, thirteen in number, were known as the "tribes" of Galway. In 1270, sixty years later than the fortifying of Athenry, its walls were built, and very soon it acquired great commercial importance, and began to be much frequented by Spanish merchants. To the intercourse with Spain are ascribed certain architectural peculiarities still to be seen among the older buildings. Some of the houses retain fantastic ornamental carvings, and many of the older buildings have a court in the centre with a gateway opening into the street.

After much fighting and suffering during the Cromwellian war, the citizens surrendered, in 1691, their Jacobite guns to the English under Ginckell, who was then passing on his way from the field of Aghrim to the "Treaty Stone" of Limerick. James Lynch Fitz-Stephen, who in 1493 was mayor, "built the choir of St. Nicholas's Church at the west end, and put painted glass in the windows." This is the famous Warden who, according to one version of the story, tried and condemned his own son, because in a fit of jealousy he murdered a rival in love. The whole of the townsfolk interceded for him, but the father, lest he should be moved from his determination, executed him with his own hands, hanging him out of a window, still pointed out in Lumbard Street, otherwise known as Dead-man's Lane. This is to be found on the north side of St. Nicholas' Church. There is a skull and cross-bones and an inscription to mark it. In the same street are some interesting old houses.

Galway is admirably situated for commercial purposes, and possesses all the natural advantages necessary for development into a first-class port. However, very great expenditure would be necessary before large steamers could use the harbour.

In 1845 exertions were made in expectation of the coming of a line of steam packets, and the huge hotel known as the Railway Hotel was built. The enterprise came to nothing, and for the last sixty years the population has steadily decreasd.

There is good salmon-fishing free on Lough Corrib, but in the town all the water below the weir is preserved. Anglers who apply for a permit for trout-fishing are usually granted it, but pay about 15s. a day to fish for salmon. Salmon abound in the River Corrib, and may often be seen from the parapet of New Bridge lying in great numbers as close together as the fingers of the hand, waiting to ascend the weir. At the spawning season this is one of the sights of Galway.

Galway presents a curious combination of dilapidation and decay, with signs of improvement and moderate prosperity. Some immense warehouses, comparatively modern, have been for several years unoccupied, and are slowly going to ruin, and in nearly every street untenanted and roofless houses suggest the "impression of a city sacked and ruined."

On many houses in the older and meaner parts of the town may be seen sculptured façades and coats-of-arms, in curious contrast with the surrounding squalor. The most entire of these antique dwellings is that known as "Lynch's Castle," in the principal street; it is really a very quaint and interesting building with fantastic carving, well-preserved, and rows of gargoyles.

The walls of the town were removed, but some portions still remain, the Lyon Tower in Eglinton Street, and the gateway at the Quay being specially worthy of notice. In the centre of the town is the spacious Eyre Square, with an enclosure laid out in walks, and planted with trees. A carved doorway, dated 1627, which once belonged to the house of a merchant, has been placed here as one of the entrances. On one side the square is occupied by the Railway Hotel and the Railway terminus, and among other buildings surrounding it are the Royal Hotel, the County of Galway Club-house, and the Bank of Ireland.

In the *Franciscan Church*, near New Bridge, which was built in the 18th century on the site of the old monastic church, are curious monuments. Notice especially that of Sir P. French, and another figured with many saints. There are some remnants of elaborate carving. Near this there once stood a Dominican Friary. It is from the *New Bridge* that you obtain quite the pleasantest view in the town.

Just beyond Lynch's Castle in Shop Street is the **Church of St. Nicholas**, dating from 1320. The tower, partly rough-cast, has uncommon corners and a modern steeple disfigured by clocks. The ornaments above the south door are peculiar. The interior was once the stables for the chargers of the Parliament troops during the Civil War. The chief features of interest are the old slabs in the south transept, and the tomb of the famous Lynch Fitz-Stephen. The font is old and good ; and in the north aisle is what is generally called " the Confessional," but "nothing is definitely known of it, and there is reason to doubt that it was ever intended for such use." There are ten bells in the tower, one of these, the old clock-bell, dated 1590, is not now used. Of the remaining nine bells the two largest are cracked. The largest bell now in use, the sixth in order of ringing, dates from 1631, and is beautifully ornamented.

University College is close to the town on the Oughterard Road. It is a fine grey limestone building standing in well-kept grounds. Museums are attached to the principal medical departments, and there is a large medical library. The belfry is a neat miniature of " Tom " Tower in Christ Church, Oxford, and unique in Ireland. The *Diocesan College* is built of the same stone, and can be seen on the way to Salthill.

The Claddagh (Irish, *Cladach*, the sea-shore or strand) is the name given to that part of Galway adjoining the harbour and inhabited chiefly by fishermen. Formerly they were a distinct community, not intermarrying with the townfolk and governed by their own magistrate or mayor, called the " King of the Claddagh," but they are now under municipal rule.

The community had at one time many singular customs. The bride received as her dowry a boat, or share of a boat, according to the means of the parents. The marriage ring was an heirloom passing from mother to daughter. It was often decorated with a heart supported by two hands. On certain days, regarded by them as unlucky, not even the presence in the bay of the most miraculous shoals of fish would tempt the fishermen to put to sea. Hardiman, in his *History of Galway*, describes this strange community, who now however conform to the manners and customs of their neighbours.

The small one-story houses are dotted about without any attempt at uniformity and present the general appearance of a bed of mushrooms.

Salthill, about a mile and a half west of Galway, is much frequented in summer on account of its sea-bathing. It is connected with Galway by tram-car, and attached to the small hotel is an extensive suite of public baths. There is a made esplanade of some two miles along the shore.

The road through Salthill continues along the coast toward Spiddle and Costelloe (see p. 218).

Galway Bay is the finest inlet on the whole Irish coast. Its length between St. Brendan's Isle and the middle of North Sound is over 30 miles, and its width at the mouth between Gorumna Island and Moher Cliffs 20 miles. Across its entrance are the three isles of Aran, stretching from north-west to south-east. Dr. Hull refers to the occurrence here of "Archæan rocks," "the most ancient of known rock-groups." Of these "the most important tract is probably that which lies along the north shore of Galway Bay." The same geologist, speaking of the glacier movements in the ice age, shows that "there was a great movement of the ice out of Galway Bay. We have here got into the great ice-stream, which was continued in a south-westerly direction along the southern shores of Galway Bay."

The **Aran Isles** (*Steamers from Galway several times a week, some of the ruins are hard to find*, see pink pages) lie in a line across the mouth of Galway Bay, about 28 miles from Galway. This excursion is one of uncommon pleasure for the ordinary tourist; for those Britons who take an intelligent

interest in the history of their own country, and the records of
the earliest pioneers of the Christian religion these "islands of
the saints" have a special fascination. As the total length
of the three islands together amounts to 14½ miles, and this
ground is more densely covered with ancient remains than any
space in Ireland of the same extent, it is clear that there is
plenty to see. We here only give a few notes upon the most
important features of the islands.

The longest island, Aranmore or North Island, is 9 miles
long and lies north-west of the others: its history is practically
that of the group. The steamer puts in at Kilronan (*Hotel:*
O'Flaherty's), the chief village.

When the mist of the past begins to lift, the earliest inhabitants that can
be descried are the Firbolgs, and when St. Enda appears, Corbanus is the
island king over a colony of pagans who seem to have come from Corcomroe,
near Ballyvaughan. The North Island, at least, had been strongly fortified
centuries before this, if we may trust our best archæologists. Enda, or
Eany, the son of Conall Deary, was brother-in-law of Aengus, King of Cashel.
Originally an abbot in Italy, he came here about the time of St. Patrick's
death (470), accepting from Aengus his gift of the North Island, and founded
one of the most important of the western seats of Christianity.

The geologist will note here the last westward records of the great ice-
sheet that seems to have descended hither from the central plain, deflected
southwards from the mountains of Connemara along the northern coast of
the bay "to such an extent that it extended all over the Aran Islands, where
Mr. Kinahan has observed striæ pointing about north 25 east" (*Hull*). The antiquarian will find here "a typical collection of nearly all of the more remarkable structures of pre-Norman times," from cromlechs and "beehive" cells
to "churches with chancels."

The uncommon characteristics of the natives mark them out as of a special
type, hardly less peculiar to the soil than the colony which Scottish tourists
find in St. Kilda. Their home-spun dress, cow-hide sandals called "pam-
pooties," and relics of ancient customs will attract notice. "We might be
disposed," says Dr. Beddoe, "trusting to Irish traditions respecting the
islands, to accept these people as representatives of the Firbolgs, had not
Cromwell, that upsetter of all things Hibernian, left in Aranmore a small
English garrison who subsequently apostatised to Catholicism, intermarried
with the natives, and so vitiated the Firbolgian pedigree." Dr. Petrie describes them as of a generally high moral character.

From the *Steamer Pier* we turn left along the bay to *Killeany*,
where of several churches only two now remain, with the lower
part only of the Round Tower. Four churches and the upper
part of the Tower were destroyed by Cromwellian soldiers to
build up the adjoining Arkin Castle. "**Enda's Chapel**" remains,
but his tomb, as his great church, have gone. Here was the

founder's chief settlement, and hither resorted Kieran of Clonmacnois, and Brendan of Smerwick before he left to cross the
howling seas and sight the "spray-swept Hebrides." The hops
found growing here may be the last survivors of the monastery
garden. On the ridge (south-east) is the "unique" oratory of
St. Benan; and south-west on the coast is the very remarkable
Black Fort, unfortunately fast disappearing.

About a mile along the western (main) road out of Kilronan
is the well-preserved *Church of Kieran*, who spent several years
with Enda. A little beyond (south-west) is DUN OGHIL, which
is considered to have been "once a finer example than Dun
Aengus" of the early fort. It is at the eastern extremity of the
central prehistoric village, *Baile na Sean*, a collection of ancient
"beehive" cells, huts and forts. About 2 miles farther along
the road is Kilmurvey. Near this (south-west) is *MacDuach's
Chapel*, named after the saint who founded the church and
tower near Gort in the 7th century. On the sea cliff, ½ mile
from the chapel, is the celebrated

DUN AENGUS, nearly 300 feet above the sea, "the central
point of interest . . . and one of the finest prehistoric
forts of Western Europe." These duns or forts, writes Miss
Stokes, are associated with the adventures of Aengus, Conor,
and "heroes of the Firbolg race. They may have been in
existence two centuries or more before the introduction of
Christianity." They were built without mortar; and the same
writer concludes that the upright jointings in the walls point to
"the work having been portioned out in lots to the labourers."
The dun here may once have had four ramparts, of which three
are now standing; and in the outer labyrinth of stones—which
rival even those on the summits of Scafell or Glyder-Fach—
we have a *cheval de frise* capable of breaking up most besieging
lines. In the doorway still remaining, with horizontal lintel
and inclined sides, we see the original type afterwards copied by
the monks; and inside one wall is the interior passage so often
found in these early forts (*e.g.* Dunbeg, Fahan).

About one mile north-west of this is another fine fort called
Dun Onaght; and near it is *Clochan na Carraige*, the most perfect
of the "beehive" cells, "formed in a manner universally adopted
by early races in all periods of the history of man and in
various portions of the globe, where stone was available, before
the knowledge of the principle of the arch had reached them. The

dome is formed by the projection of one stone beyond another till the walls meet in one flag at the apex " (*M. Stokes*). The *Church of St. Brecan* is only ½ mile to the north and is worth a visit. This, which without reason is called the "Seven Churches," was probably founded by Brecan, the 6th-century bishop who founded Ardbrecan (Meath) and several churches in County Clare. It contains a very early window in the north wall ; and once had a monastery on the north side. Observe the inscription, "VII *ro-ma-ni,*" on a stone to the south-west, which proves the extensive reputation of the monastery ; the broken headstone of St. Brecan's grave ; and, higher up, the broken but splendidly carved cross. The "Saint's Bed " is pointed out.

INISHMAAN, or Middle Island, is divided by Gregory Sound, about 1¼ mile in width. *Dun Conor*, named after the brother of Aengus, is of a curious oval shape, and, though terribly "restored," is a fine fort. The story of Mailly, the murderer, should be learnt from a native. *Teampull Murry* [1] (St. Mary's Church) is of 15th-century date. The saint *Kenerg*, whose " bed " is here, was the brother of the lady Cavanagh to whom the *Kenanagh Church*, with an uncommon west door, may be dedicated.

On SOUTH ISLAND, the most interesting of several early ruins, is *St. Cavan's Church*, named after the brother of Kevin of Glendalough, and the disciple of Enda.

[The literature dealing with the islands is extensive. The general tourist will find an excellent and illustrated description in the *R.S.A.I. Handbook*, No. II., by T. J. Westropp (Hodges, 1s.)· For others, Lord Dunraven's ' Notes'" will prove exhaustive.]

GALWAY TO THE BURREN OF CLARE, BALLYVAUGHAN, LISDOONVARNA, THE CLIFFS OF MOHER AND KILKEE.

Steamer three times a week to Ballyvaughan. Railway—The West Clare Railway, reached from Galway by Ennis Junction.

The Burren of Clare, to the north of Lisdoonvarna, is formed chiefly of terraced hills, rising gradually to a height of from 800 to 1000 feet. They are composed entirely of bare limestone rock of pale gray colour—the carboniferous limestone of geologists. The beds rise very gently from beneath the coal-measure shales, and end in steep slopes looking down upon Galway Bay. Blackhead forms one of the principal of these slopes. Deep valleys

---

[1] The absence of this among the names of patron saints, or upon the crosses and tombs of those early churches before the Norman Invasion, is remarkable.

penetrate this high limestone ground both from Galway Bay on the north and from the low country on the east, towards which a line of lofty cliffs looks down, like those on the north, and extends in a wavy line from near Kinvarra to near Corrofin.

Glen Columbkill is the most remarkable of the valleys on the east of the Burren high land. What makes those valleys so remarkable is the bareness of the limestone rocks which surround them. They look like vast artificial amphitheatres rising in regular steps and terraces of stone, receding here and advancing there, till the long parallel lines of stratification fade away in the blue haze of the distance. The isolated hills are like great fortifications surrounded by regular bastions and walls rising one above another, till each terminates in a small citadel crowning the summit of the hill. The light gray of the nearer hills fades into purple in the distance, and, should a stray sunbeam strike through the clouds on some remoter promontory, the part lit gleams out like a marble building, with all the effect of some magnificent architecture.

The numerous rock fissures are lined with the most splendid ferns and other plants—the delicate maidenhair fern being found here as well as on the Aran Islands, together with several species of plants very rarely to be met with in other parts of the British Islands.

From BALLYVAUGHAN (*Hotels:* (C.) Kerin's ; Mrs. Davis'), 7 miles eastward along the Bay, is Corcomroe Abbey, an offshoot of the great monastery of Furness in Lancashire. It was founded about 1182 by a king of Limerick, Donaldmore O'Brien, and dedicated to St. Mary.[1] Though rude in structure as seen to-day, ancient accounts tell of "the purple marble and polished stones, starry ornaments and whitewashed walls of the Abbey." The cloister-square and church still remain. In the chancel of the church there are the altar, the sedilia, and the most interesting object of the building—the large figure of *King Conor Roe O'Brien* (1267), grandson of the founder, which gives a sculptured record of the royal Irish dress of the 13th century.

A public car from Lisdoonvarna meets the steamer at Ballyvaughan.

Lisdoonvarna (*Hotels:* * Thomond House ; Queen's ; Imperial ;

---

[1] There is a good description of the abbey and this part of Clare in *R.S.A.I. Handbook*, No. II., by T. J. Westropp.

(I.A.C., C.) Atlantic View ; Royal Spa ; Kincona ; Glenbourne ; Lynch's) is one of the most frequented spas of Ireland, and increasing in popularity.   It is not in any way a tourist resort, but extraordinarily beneficial to invalids, especially those suffering from arthritis and rheumatism.   Springs of iron, sulphur and with chalybeate qualities have been discovered.   The "twin-springs" of iron and sulphur rise within a few inches of each other.   There is a pump-house and public bath-house, and at some of the hotels, as at Thomond House, there are special arrangements for hot-air baths and electric baths for special cures.   Thomond House is not exactly an hotel, but resembles the hydropathic establishments so popular in Scotland.   It is famed for its flowers, and, under the management of its pro-prietress, Mrs. Bulger, a lady well-known in society, is achieving a unique position.   Terms from 3 guineas a week.

The whole district is a botanist's paradise, and in many of the rocks here and on the sea-coast are sheltered crevices which by their retained heat foster many rare specimens.

To the sea-shore westward, where sea-bathing may be had, the distance is only 4 miles.   County Clare abounds in ancient ruins, any one of which would make the fortune of an English resort.   **Kilfenora**, about 5 miles south-east of Lisdoonvarna, is of interest from its remarkable high cross and ruined church. At Dysart O'Dea are other interesting ruins.

Ennistymon (8 miles) on the West Clare Railway is the station for Lisdoonvarna.   Before reaching it the line from Ennis passes Corofin with beautiful Lough Inchiquin with the ridge of Keentlea, the "serpents' hill" rising above it.

Ennistymon (several hotels) is rather a quaint little place, and with its river and falls has some character.   The "great" house is that of H. V. Macnamara, Esq.

The next station is Lehinch (*Hotels :* (I.A.C.) "Golf Links," *of the "late Norwegian style of architecture*; (C.) Kerin's Aberdeen Arms, *comfortable*).   In itself calling for little remark the place is well known on account of its excellent golf-links, 18 holes, laid out on the sandhills by Liscannor Bay.   The large hotel aims at exclusiveness, which is delightful for those who can afford it.

The "lion" of the district is the CLIFFS OF MOHER (6 miles). To gain them follow the road round the bay northward through Liscannor and on until a road at right angles leads straight

as a line uphill to a column with a figure on the summit.
Thence take left at next fork and pass St. Bridget's Holy Well.
It is all uphill. Continue until a curious ruin is seen in a field
on the left. Then pass through a gate to it; cycles and motors
may be left here, and a short walk of ½ mile over easy grass
brings us to the head of the cliffs capped by O'Brien's Tower.
Few cliffs worth seeing are as easily accessible. Slabs of slate
are so arranged as to reassure the most nervous, and by looking
over this "railing" we may see a glorious view. The cliffs
themselves are 600 feet in height and almost vertical. Only by
noting the diminutiveness of a boat below can we gauge the real
altitude. Black as ink in places and studded by countless sea-
birds, their grandeur and solemnity is remarkable. The crags
below add to the scene, and away to sea the Isles of Aran are
spread out like a map between us and the distant mountains of
Connemara.

From Lehinch the railway goes southward to **Milltown
Malbay.** About 2 miles south of this is Spanish Point, where
several vessels of the Spanish Armada were wrecked. After
this the scenery calls for no remark. At Doonbeg the railway
turns inland to Moyasta junction for Kilkee and Kilrush
(see p. 196).

THE WESTERN HIGHLANDS OF CONNEMARA.

I. Galway to Recess and Clifden by railway. From Recess or Clifden to Westport by road, visiting on the way Kylemore, Killery, Leenane and Dhulough.

II. Galway to Lough Corrib and Cong ; road from Cong by Maam to Maam Cross Station, where the train may be joined for Recess or Clifden ; or direct from Cong to Leenane ; or from Cong to Ballinrobe station.

ROUTE I.

GALWAY TO CLIFDEN BY RAILWAY : THENCE TO WESTPORT BY ROAD.

As the road is closely followed by the railway, and the cyclist, though on good surface, will often meet with hindering winds rather than beautiful scenery until he reaches Recess, we confine our remarks to the railway.

Leaving the large station of Galway, we notice one of the chief features of the town, the curious and top-heavy tower of the R.C. Church, bristling with pinnacles. Then after backing inland a short way, we make for the wilds of Connemara across the flat-banked river Corrib. As the line steers midway between that river and, on the left side, the thickly wooded hills, Menlough Castle (see p. 236) with perhaps a straggling cow or a sunburnt turf-cutter, are the only varieties along some miles of monotony.

CONNEMARA is the western section of County Galway, cut off on the east and north by Lough Corrib, Lough Mask, and Killery Harbour, and bounded on the west by the sea. It has many and varied attractions. It possesses, perhaps, few treasures for the archæologist, and perchance the golfer may too often find the coffee-room carpet his only putting-green, but the walker no less than the artist who explores the beauties of Ballynahinch, the Killery, and the coast, will find some of the finest scenes in Erin ; the angler in a happy season, who whips

Inishdegil Mꞇe

Mweelrea
2688

Uggool

Crump I.

ky Rocks

Freaghillaun

Shanvallybeg

Lit Killary

Funskoge Quay 1823

Maumore

Renvyle Pt

Renvyle Ho.

Renvyle Ho.

Carrickabullog Rocks

Inishbroon

Church

Ardnagreevagh

Renvyle Inn

Cloonagh

L. Muck

Casheen

Renvyle Hotel

Tully L.

Gowlaun

Benchoona 1312

Letter-Boy 1172

Renvyle Hill

R.C.C. Tully Cross

873

Garraun 1973

Freghillaun S.

Derryinver

Ballynakill

Doo Ros R.

Dawros R.

Douehruagh 1736

Kylemore Castle

Lit Kylemore Ho.

18

Tower

Cleggan

Shanboolard Hall

C.G.Sta

Ross Ho.

Doghus Beg

Sch.

Pollacappul

Kylemore L.

92

Cleggan

Ballynakill L.

Crockaguroe

Rosleague

Quay

Hotel

Letterfrack

Knocklurack 1460

Benbrack

Kylemore Knu.

ghduff

Shinnanagh

Moyard

Traheen Br.

Diamond Hill 1460

Altnowerty

758

agh 384

L. Tanny

L. Naguroge

Muckanoght

Benbaun

The Twelve

Doon Cas

L. Nagaun

700

L. Nahillion

Tievebaun 1810

Townaloughra

Benbreen 2276

Kingstown Bay

Shanakeever

L. Anna

Owennliu R.

Bengower 1181

CLIFDEN

Ardbear

C O N

Derryclea

N

Ardbear Bay

Monastery

Derryclea L.

Island L.

Lettershea

Benlettery

Ballynahinch

Drumneen

Salt

Munga

Emlaghmore

Holy Well

Mannin Bay

Ballinaboy

Ballinaboy Br.

Cloonagal

Conga L.

Ballynahinch Sta.

Ballinafad

45

L. Nabruc

Emlaghnabeg

Fadda

Agh L.

Scannive

Toombeola Br.

Toombeola

Clogmisle

Ballyconeely

L. Inaserd

Errismore

Boolagar

Nasoodery

Naweelaun

Cushatrower

Aillenacally

Bunowen

Forglass

L. Bollard

Letterdife Ho.

Rosroe L.

Ballyconeely Bay

Maumeen L.

Roundstone

Urrisbeg 987

Inishnee

Maumgor

Hen I.

Urrisbeg West

Ervallagh

Bertraghbo Bay

Carrickaloughaun Rocks

Gorteen

Quay

Inishlackan

Knockboy 360

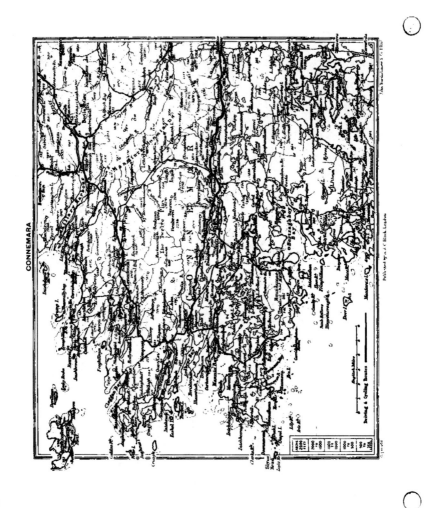

CONNEMARA

the loughs and streams south of Lough Inagh, will have every variety of water and probably good sport ; whilst to those that climb,—without hands,—the Twelve Bens and the Maamturks afford abundance of good mountaineering. The botanist will find nature bountiful here, and to the geologist she is more than generous. Lastly for the man on wheels we need not do more than quote the opinion of Mr. Mecredy, who declares it "a cyclist's paradise."

Geologically the district is conveniently divided into halves by the Galway-Clifden Railway, which marks off the Silurian mountains of the north from the important tract of the oldest or "Archæan" rocks of the southern side. Dr. E. Hull refers to the strong resemblance of this wild southern tract to "some tracts in Sutherlandshire formed of rocks of the same age." He draws attention to the numerous rock basins and moraine-dammed loughs ; "a glance at the Ordnance or larger geological maps will illustrate this better than any description." Some tracts of the country, such as those lying to the south of Clifden and bordering Kilkerrin Bay, are a perfect network of loughlets, ice-worn bosses of rock, and hummocky mounds of drift. "These basins and loughlets," he states, "cannot be accounted for by any other theory than that of glacial agency."

For the origin of the name of Connemara we turn to Dr. Joyce, who explains that Maeve—the famous queen of Connaught in the first century A.D., and the "Mab" of English folk-lore— had three sons, of whom the second was named *Conmac.* The descendants of this prince all settled in Connaught and were called Conmac-*ne.* One of their districts lay near the sea and was called "Conmae-ne-*mara,* or the 'sea-side'—Conmacne, which has been shortened to the present name Con-ne-mara."

Beyond *Moycullen* station (7¾ miles) Knocknalee Hill is a pleasing feature in the left-hand distance, and to avoid it the rail keeps low, and near to Lough Ross. Three miles past Ross station the ruins of *Aughnanure Castle* are seen on the right. This was the ancient seat of the O'Flahertys, whose modern house is *Lemonfield.*

In the 13th century the O'Flahertys, being driven from their possessions on the east side of Lough Corrib by the De Burgos, sailed across the lake and drove out the possessors of the territory there, and became powerful enough in this part of Conne-mara to prove a thorn in the side of the English authorities,

with whom they were continually at war. Though doubtless a
very ancient feudal castle once occupied the site, the portions of
the building still left do not indicate an earlier date than the
16th century. Of the castle, the strong square keep and barti-
zan remain, with indications of the banqueting-room and various offices. The interiors of the windows of the banqueting-hall
are worthy of notice, on account of the decorative stone carving
they display.

Oughterard (*Hotels*. (C.) Angler's ; Railway ; (I.A.C.)
Murphy's ; Monaghan), about 17 miles from Galway, is a well-
known fishing centre. There is a fish-hatchery here. A little
distance from the town, near the bridge, the river forms a
series of pretty cascades, called the Falls of Feogh. The valley
is well planted, and is more sheltered by trees than most of
the bare hillsides of this district.

The attractive form of Carrigogue soon comes out on the
right ; behind which, high up are, so tradition saith, the Bed
and Holy-Well of St. Patrick. At *Maam Cross Station* (26½
miles), a direct north and south road crosses the line, going
(north) to Maam Bridge, and Leenane (p. 226), and south to
Screeb Bridge.

It is 6 miles south to Screeb Bridge and another 6 miles by a
straight road, to the *Costello river*, on Costello (*pron.* "Cashla")
Bay, where there is a little hotel which offers good white trout
fishing. Eastward, beyond this, a pretty regular line of coast
is followed closely by the road to Galway. At 11½ miles from
Galway is *Spiddle* (Inn), where the Owenboliska river can be
fished ; and several streams, such as the Ballynew, Awinriff,
and Loughkip, are crossed by this road west of Spiddle.

Turning west from Costello we should come to an archipelago
of islands in Kilkieran Bay. Five of the largest are joined by
bridges, relief work done when Rt. Hon. G. W. Balfour was
Irish Secretary. At *Lettermullen* is the Hotel of the Isles
where brown trout and sea trout fishing and rough shooting
are offered to visitors. Some of these small out-of-the-way
hotels are both comfortable and reasonable, and deserve to be
better known.

At 33 miles from Galway is Recess, where we stop first at the
small station belonging to the splendid hotel of the M.G.W.R.
Company ; and, one mile beyond, reach the principal station.

RECESS.

RAILWAY STATIONS.—See just above.
HOTELS.—(I.A.C.) *Recess*, Midland Great Western Railway Company.
    Cashel (Zetland Arms), 6 miles (see p. 221).

The fame of Recess, doubtless increasing every year, is due to its advantage as a centre for fishing or exploring the fine fishery district of Ballynahinch, at the foot of the "Twelve Bens." The Railway Hotel, with a platform of its own, stands in beautiful grounds, and is in the first rank for comfort.

To the fisherman and the scenery-hunter alike this district is, in the words of an enthusiast, "a dream of pleasure." It is pre-eminently an angler's resort, and, indeed, one of the best fishing centres in Ireland. The two principal fisheries are the "*Ballynahinch*" and "*Gowla*" or "*Cashel*" Fisheries. For latter see below. The principal waters of the "Ballynahinch" are the lough and river of that name, also Loughs Glendalough, Inagh, Derryclare, and Oorid. Visitors staying at the hotel are allowed free fishing on all of the above waters which lie east of the hotel down to where the Owentovey and Recess rivers join, and occasionally beats may be rented at £1 a day in Ballynahinch Lough, etc. Full information from Mr. A. Mathews, Estate Office, Ballynahinch. Salmon begin running in spring, the big run taking place in June and July. Sea-trout run in July and August.

Lough Ballynahinch, together with the north-eastern loughs of Derryclare and Inagh, its feeders, curves crescent-wise round the eastern feet of the Twelve Bens. Thackeray in his enthusiasm declared that the beauty here rivalled that of Killarney.

"I won't attempt," he wrote, "to pile up big words in place of those wild mountains, over which the clouds as they passed, or the sunshine as it went and came, cast every variety of tint, light and shadow ; nor can it be expected that long level sentences, however smooth and shining, can be made to pass as representations of those calm lakes by which we took our way. All one can do is to lay down the pen and ruminate, and cry 'Beautiful!' once more ; and to the reader say 'Come and see!'"

The feature *par excellence* of this part of the country, a thing of beauty indeed, of which the tourist never tires, is the splendid group of **The Bens**, which raise here their noble peaks "in the heart of some of the loveliest scenery in the world, full of varied and interesting scrambles, and botanically are pre-eminently the richest in mountain plants in Connaught" (*M. C. Hart*). The geologist will find in these mountains the same "*quartzite rising in great arches or folds, which after disappearing northwards for some 20 miles, rises again in Croagh Patrick on Clew Bay.* Sometimes the sides of these hills are destitute of vegetation, where it cannot cling to the dry gritty substance. They have also undergone considerable polishing from former glacial action ; so that it will be easily understood how, seen from certain directions and under favourable sunlight, the mountain sides glisten like glass, or rather with the rich yellowish hue of burnished gold." The views of the Bens which to us appear most striking are those obtained from the road along the eastern shore of Lough Inagh ; from this are clearly seen the three successive "shoulders," like rounded cushions, which rise from the island-studded lake buttressing up the tapering peaks above. Bengorm, 2336 feet high, forms a very graceful summit, but the loftiest point of the group is Benbaun, which is 2395 feet.

At Recess is the principal quarry of the famous ornamental stone known as *Connemara Marble*, described by Dr. Hull as composed of "crystalline limestone and serpentine." Those who have seen the pillars and facings of the Entrance Hall at the New Geological Museum of Trinity College, Dublin, will remember the beautiful green colouring of this exquisite rock. There is also a magnificent specimen in the Natural History department of the Dublin Museum.

There is a rich treat for the cyclist on the way from Recess Station to Kylemore. This is a run of 13 miles along the splendid road that goes northwards round the curving shores of Loughs Derryclare and INAGH. The latter is one of the finest bits of scenery to be found in Ireland, especially when one is lucky enough to get sunshine on the eastern shoulders of the "Bens" after rain. For the character of this view of those mountains, see remarks on page 219. The only vegetation is on the islands. For Kylemore see page 226.

The "GOWLA' or CASHEL FISHERY is leased by Mr. O'Loghlen, the proprietor of the *Zetland Arms Hotel* (I.A.C.), Cashel, situated from 2 to 3 miles from the Gowla river and 5 miles from Recess Station. This is pre-eminently an Anglers' hotel, and those who are enthusiasts will thoroughly appreciate

THE TWELVE PINS, CONNEMARA.

it. The hotel was built as a private residence by the father of the present proprietor, and afterwards enlarged as its popularity increased. (Terms from £2 : 15s. per week.) There are 8 beats for rods, including those on the most beautiful little Lough Anilaun. The charge for a day's ticket is 10s. ; weekly ticket £2 : 10s. Boat and man 2s. 6d. a day. To visitors at Cashel Hotel the brown and white trout fishing on the Gowla-beg stream (4 *to 7 miles south*) is free. There is rough shooting over 15,000 acres.

About 12 miles south of Cashel is *Carna* (Morgan's Hotel), with good sea-fishing.

Railway Route continued : — After Recess **Ballynahinch Station** comes next.

It is a walk of about 1½ mile from the station to the church by the delightful road that passes Ballynahinch House, and from the rising ground you will find some of the most charming little views in Ireland, if not indeed in the kingdom. There is just enough foliage to make a rich foreground, and through the opening trees the old ruined tower of the castle stands black against the silvery lake that washes the feet of the graceful slopes of Bengower. The easel and the brush have already penetrated thus far, and this land of beauty is not unknown on the walls of "Burlington House." This was for centuries the seat of the Martins, a powerful family in feudal times. It was a common phrase among the peasantry that "Colonel Martin was the best Martin that ever *reigned*," clearly denoting the almost regal power of the family, who possessed about 200,000 acres of ground in this country. Charles Lever's book, *The Martins of Cro-Martin*, deals with this family.

On the west arm of Bertraghboy Bay, 7 miles south of Ballynahinch, is *Roundstone* (*Hotels:* Mellet ; (C.) Kinton (temp.)), one of the most health-giving resorts on the west coast. The view from the town is of considerable grandeur, the mountains seeming to rise from the sea. Rare botanical plants grow in profusion on Urrisbeg, and the purple blossoms of the gentian are seen everywhere. The place is very popular with artists. Within a mile of the town lie Gurteen Beaches and Dog's Bay which present a fine and safe bathing-place and are well worthy of a visit. In the summer there are two incoming mails daily.

At the south end of Bertraghboy Bay lies *St. Macdara's Island*, 6 miles by sea from Roundstone. It can be also reached from Carna, some 5 miles west of Kilkieran pier. This to the archæologist is the most interesting island between High Island and the Arans. It contains at the east point "one of the most typical of the ancient ecclesiastical structures we possess," and one that "in some respects has no fellow." "The different features of this *church* point strongly to a 7th-century erection" (*F. T. Biggar*). The stone roof, of which much remains, is the best example of this kind of work extant. Though the island is now uninhabited there is evidence that Saint Sinach ("the fox"), *alias* MacDara, settled here in the 6th or 7th century and built this chapel of cyclopean masonry. Fish and "kelp" must, we take it, have been a pretty common dish on the table of his "establishment."

Beyond Ballynahinch the line runs through a wild and rugged district giving a splendid view of the Twelve Pins About half way to Clifden a glimpse is caught of the tall poles of the Marconi installation at Mannin Bay.

Clifden (*Hotels:* (C.) Lyden's; (I.A.C., C.) Railway; M'Donnell's). The town is dusty and uninteresting; so late as the year 1815 there was only a single house on the site. Its origin is due to Mr. D'Arcy, who first pointed out the advantageous position, and offered " leases for ever, together with four acres of mountain land, at but a short distance from the projected town, at twenty shillings per annum." Clifden is favourably situated on a ridge at the head of the Bay of Ardbear, near the Atlantic coast, of which a fine view may be had from the neighbouring hills. The Owenglen river makes a picturesque cascade close to the town.

The little town is overwhelmed both by the monster Workhouse and the huge Roman Catholic Cathedral. The latter has indeed a handsome spire; but both these buildings are out of all proportion to the population here.

At the head of the two bays of Ardbear and Mannin, south of Clifden, are the well-known *oyster beds* belonging to Mr. Corless of Dublin.

CLIFDEN CASTLE, formerly belonging to the D'Arcys, stands about 2 miles up the bay. "After reaching the entrance of the harbour of Clifden, and rounding a promontory, the castle comes into view. It is in a ruinous state, but stands in a fine situation. Mountain and wood rise behind, and a fine sloping lawn in front reaches down to the land-locked bay, while to the right the eye ranges over the ocean until it mingles with the far and dim horizon." The D'Arcys, who had done so much to improve this portion of Connemara, became so reduced by their liberality as to be compelled to sell their property.

Continuing the road past the castle, we may round the headland and return by Kingstown, where a boat may be hired to visit—

HIGH ISLAND (or ARDILAUN). This uninhabited island, the romantic home of St. Feichin and his monks, was explored by Petrie and has been well described in the *R.S.A.I. Journal*, 1896, by Mr. Macalister, from whom we borrow. Not far from Castlepollard, amid the bog-lands of Westmeath, there are at Fore the interesting remains of the once important religious settlement of Saint Feichin. This vigorous monk was the first to preach the Gospel to the wild westerns of Galway, and at Omey and on High Island he raised churches and cells. "We may perhaps regard ourselves as tolerably correct if we assign 630-640 as about the date of the foundation of the latter." Gormgall, "the blue-eyed foreigner," probably lived here and died on Ardillaun in 1017.

The island is only accessible in calm weather, and then the landing (at the north-east) is difficult. The CHAPEL, the principal ruin, is at the south end near the larger loughlet. As it is 3 feet longer than Molaise's Chapel on Inismurray, it is not quite the smallest chapel in the British Isles. The lintel over the west door was once a "monumental cross," and the most interesting cross here is on the south side. Since Petrie's day the place has been shamefully destroyed; the cells or *clochans* of the monastery have suffered much, and only two now stand. Though the existence of the monks' *mill* may be disputed, the pilgrims' offerings sufficiently indicate the ancient fame of the Holy Well, in the centre of the island.

CLIFDEN TO WESTPORT.

[For car arrangements see *pink pages*.]

Our road, which leaves Clifden at the west end of the Roman Catholic Church, is at first through a wild and rocky country, but the glimpses of mountain ravines, the varied views of the Atlantic, and the alternation of hill and valley, contribute to the interest of a very fine route, of which, however, the first part is the best.

As far as Moyard (6 miles) take all the main turns to the right. The road is usually stony, no roller being used.

About 2 miles from Clifden we get a fine view of Kingstown Bay and the islands of Turbot and Lesser Inishturk to W.S.W., and a mile farther on we see Cleggan Head, Tower, and Bay, and the islands of Inishbofin and Inishark to the north-west. About 4½ miles from Clifden we arrive at the crest of a hill, from which a magnificent view is obtained of the valley in which Letterfrack is situated, and of the Kylemore Mountains which close it in. From this point there is a very fine sight of the "Twelve Pins" standing out boldly. We have, in one grand panorama, not only the Bens, but also a wide valley stretching

far ahead, in part a great brown waste of moorland, studded
with farmsteads and cabins, and bright spots in the midst of
the sombre hues, showing the gleam of lakes of various sizes
and shapes ; a splendid arm of the sea (Ballynakill Harbour),
almost completely land-locked ; a magnificent mountain promontory, tinted with silver, grays, purples, and browns ; and
away 12 miles north-east is Mweelrea over Killery Harbour.

A little beyond Ballynakill Church and Renton (6 miles) we
bear left, and then past the little pier in full view of the graceful
cone of Diamond Mountain.

Letterfrack (9 miles ; *Hotel :* O'Grady's). This little village,
well-nigh buried in fuchsias, is one of the sweetest bits in
all Ireland, and vies with Ballynahinch for first place as the
sketcher's favourite haunt in Connemara.

It lies at the foot of mountains of no common form and
beauty, and possesses a good hotel.

A most enjoyable road of 5 miles goes from Letterfrack northwards by Ballynakill Harbour and Tully crossroads to Renvyle.
The coast scenery about and beyond the coastguard station is
magnificent. The sea is studded with islands and rocks of all
sorts and sizes ; straight ahead is the lofty hill on Clare Island,
with Inishturk and many another "Inis" to the left; far
behind them in the distance Croaghaun and Slievemore lift
their shapely summits in Achill Island ; while, to the right,
Mweelrea, the aged sentinel of Killery Harbour, rises over
Salruck.

Mrs. Blake's Hotel, Renvyle House (£3 per week), is most
homely and comfortable, besides being unique ; for its walls,
within, retain their antique elm and oak wainscotting, and it
lies as snugly embowered as some old English "grange." The
hostess's family bought the property in 1680, some time after
Cromwell had confiscated their ancient home. (See *The Blake
Records* published by Elliot Stock.) There is a famous library
with many seventeenth and eighteenth century books, including
a first edition of Raleigh's *History of the World.* There is
brown trout fishing and also sea-fishing free except for boat.
There is a golf course and some mixed shooting, and the easel
of the marine artist is often to be seen on the shore. With all
these attractions it is small wonder that Renvyle is popular.

The hotel stands on Lough Renvyle (fresh water), close to

the sea, and from Renvyle Hill (1572 feet) there is a splendid view over the Atlantic and the many islands along the coast, as far north as the Clare Island in Clew Bay and the distant hills of Achill. About a mile from the hotel are the ruins of Renvyle Castle, with old church and well.

A frequent excursion from Letterfrack or from Renvyle is to SALRUCK. Through Tully Cross Roads, 3 miles north of Letterfrack, continue along the pleasant coast-road to the slated house on Lough Muck (*cyclists can leave their machines here*). From this a roughish track turns sharply left and makes a steep descent to Salruck, a beautiful wooded spot on a wild bit of coast. There is a curious graveyard here where the graves are covered with stones and adorned with clay pipes, a fact which has led some superficial observers to conclude that the natives made votive offerings to the dead. As a matter of fact at the "wakes" pipes are handed round, and afterwards collected and placed on the graves.

Returning to the slated house, turn left and keep the road that skirts the north side of Lough Fee. From the point where this strikes the main road it is 6 miles (left) to Leenane, and 9 (right) to Letterfrack.

Thus we pass along Killery which means "red valley" and the name is well-deserved, as the rocks on every side have a curious, reddish-purple tinge, giving the impression of blooming heather. Also here, more than elsewhere, a rich red dye for their home-spun woollen is in great favour with women and girls, and many a fine view is touched up in the foreground by a flaming bit of colour. The local industries are crochet-lace and tweeds, specimens of which, both in the process of manufacture and as the finished article, can be seen at Leenane.

The direct road (*good cycling*) from Letterfrack to Leenane, a distance of 12½ miles, after passing the Post Office, and for a mile and a half, consists of an avenue of fuchsias of unusual height and flower. We have never seen this shrub growing in greater luxuriance in our islands; not even in the Port Erin country in the Isle of Man. The air at Letterfrack is of that mild freshness characteristic of the neighbourhood. The little town lies between the Twelve Pins and the sea.

The beautiful Diamond Hill is away on the right; and from its eastern shoulder tumbles the Dawros stream, which the road soon crosses. Then, at about 2¼ miles from the Post Office, you

enter one of the most charming bits in all this land of inter-
mittent beauty—the demesne of **Kylemore** (*admission to grounds
granted on application*). By a bridge you cross a stream
which falls and glitters through the crowded copse. Here are
trees of every timber—holly, fir, ash and birch ; around you the
blossoms of fuchsia, laurestinus and rhododendron are seen
in profusion ; whilst above, the slopes of Kylemore Hill roll
mantled in foliage to the Castle lawn.

A little past the church, and 5 miles from Letterfrack, the
wild road from Lough Inagh and Recess comes in on the right ;
2¾ miles beyond (left) the main road is joined by the road just
described from Salruck and Renvyle ; then we approach the
southern shore of the GREAT KILLERY, which is touched at the
inn opposite Bundorragh "Quay."

A *Ferry Boat* is sometimes to be had at this inn for the opposite shore and
Dhulough ; but the hotel boat from Leenane is commonly used, unless the
whole circuit of the head of the bay at Aasleagh be made by the road. The
latter is a round of 10½ miles.

Two miles of good road brings us to

LEENANE.

NEAREST RAILWAY STATIONS.—*Maam Cross* (13 miles); *Recess* (17½ miles);
 Clifden (20½ miles); *Westport* (31¼ miles; or by Louisburgh, 35 miles).

HOTEL.—(I.A.C., C.) M'Keown's.

CARS.—In summer, to Westport and Clifden. See *pink pages.*

DISTANCES.—Kylemore, 8 ; Renvyle, 17 ; Salruck, 8 ; Letterfrack, 11½ ;
 Aasleagh, 2 ; Erriff Bridge, 7¾ ; Nafooey, 10 ; Delphi, 10½ ; Dhulough,
 11¼ ; Louisburgh, 21 ; Cong, 27.

If one were to select the half-dozen best hotels in Ireland,
Leenane would certainly be included. It combines in itself the
freedom from conventionality which is such a powerful attraction to town workers on holiday, and the comforts of an up-to-
date hostelry. The terms are also unusually reasonable. The
situation is magnificent. It stands on the very edge of the
great Killery inlet, and is backed up by rising hills. Towering
opposite are the heights of Bengorm (2303 ft.). Looking seaward

the sunsets over Mweelrea (2688 ft.), and Benbury (2610 ft.) are a thing to be remembered, and inland rises the quaintly named "Devil's Mother" (2131 ft.).

Leenane is a half-way house between Clifden and Westport. It is in a particularly favourable position for excursions (see below). There is bathing in the lough close to the hotel. There is salmon and white trout fishing in Culfin River and certain loughs at 5s. a day; brown trout free fishing in several rivers and loughs, and of course the sea-fishing is free. There is mixed shooting on the bay. It is one of the sights of Leenane to see the fishermen draw in their nets full of struggling silver salmon along the shores in the mornings. Mr. M'Keown of the hotel is one of the well-known landlord-proprietors, not uncommon in Ireland, who by their personality go far to contribute to the success of their enterprises.

The valley of the Erriff river, which at Leenane is deepened and widened into the Greater Killery or "red fiord," is of considerable interest to the geologist, who will doubtless have at hand the descriptions of Harkness and Hull. It is sufficient here to remind the general tourist that in this remarkable inlet, 12 miles in length, "the *glacial phenomena* are very striking," and the rocks are "scored with groovings pointing down the valley, while masses of moraine matter with huge boulders are strewn along the shore," and that, like the Estuary of the Shannon and Cork harbour, it was, during the Ice Age, a much shallower valley, and a "channel of fresh water." Old "Mountain *terraces*" may be seen on the sides of the Delphi valley, and along the road to Cong; and at the head of the harbour the lines of "river terraces" are easily observed. Sheets of lava and ash visible along the south shore-road are proofs of *volcanic action*.

Of the two favourite excursions that to KYLEMORE, if not already included in the journey from the west, is the most popular (see p. 226).

To AASLEAGH, the hamlet at the head of the Killery, it is a little over 2 miles, and Aasleagh Lodge Waterfall is a local "lion." Five miles higher up the valley, along the direct *Westport Road*, is

ERRIFF BRIDGE. "A beautiful salmon river," says Hi-Regan of the Erriff; it is a stream which forms a good centre for the fisherman, and is fed by the Owenduff stream and the Tanyard Lough, in which the latter rises, and by the Glendawaugh, and other higher rivers. Southwards, the Partry Mountains supply fishing waters in Lough Nafooey and the Upper Aille, well known to worm-baiters.

At the divergence of the road to MAAM CROSS, a little above the hotel, there is a justly popular view of the "fiord" seen from the foot of *Devil's Mother Mountain* (2131)—a hill which ought to repay the climber with good views. This road, which passes through the heart of the Joyce country, meets (5½ miles) the road from Lough Nafooey, and its waterfall, and Cong (page 236).

LOUGH NAFOOEY is a beautiful sheet of water, and quite one of the best bits in this district. It can be reached in 10 miles by turning up the road referred to just above.

The JOYCE COUNTRY comprehends the north of the county of Galway, including in its area Killery, part of Lough Corrib, Lough Mask, and the group of the Maamturk Mountains. The first Joyce is said to have come to Ireland in the reign of Edward I., and acquired extensive property in Jar-Connaught. The Joyces have the reputation of being the tallest and strongest race in Ireland.

In MWEELREA (2688 feet), the noble mountain "which stands like a great watch-tower guarding the entrance to Killery Harbour," the Upper Silurian grits and conglomerates rise to their highest point in the west of Ireland. It is well worth ascending for the splendid views obtained : the hotel boatman is a good authority on the most convenient place for a start.

The most interesting route to Westport, 31¼ miles, that *via* Louisburgh, can be followed through Aasleagh (*good cycling*), or met by the hotel ferry at a point 1⅓ mile east of Bundorragh Quay. This route was at first followed by the Railway motor cars, but latterly they have taken the shorter and much less interesting way direct to Westport on account of the better surface.

DELPHI LODGE, built by the late Marquis of Sligo on the site of the old house, is beautifully situated on the small Finlough. It stands on a rocky ledge in the midst of a fine group of Scotch firs. The little waterfall on the north side of the house is often visited by tourists, who will find no difficulty in obtaining the necessary permission. Finlough, with Dhulough (the black lake), about ¾ mile distant, and' the river which flows into the Killery at Bundorragh, form perhaps the most perfect ideal of a salmon and trout fishery in the kingdom. The lessee of the Lodge, with all sporting rights,

is the Rev. E. Spencer Gough, rector of Barningham, Yorkshire.
The road from Leenane around by Aasleagh and Delphi to the
upper end of Dhulough offers a delightful cycling run, and
includes some mountain and sea views not to be surpassed in
the British Isles. During the Royal tour in Ireland, in 1903,
the King of Greece paid a special visit to Delphi, Princess
Victoria and the Lord-Lieutenant spending some time in fishing
the river and lake, the Royal party afterwards taking tea at the
Lodge. The house overlooking Dhulough is an attractive
feature on going through the Delphi pass. It was here that
Walsham How, the late Bishop of Wakefield, died while on a
fishing holiday in 1897. The road which branches off to the right
just below Dhulough is a rather rough road, but the views of
Tanyard Lake, and in the Sheffry Pass, are of a wild, and it
might be said, magnificent character. It is the most attractive
route from Delphi, and also the shorter to Westport, and is by
no means impassable for a carriage and pair. The district is
known as the Barony of Murrisk, a very ancient name, a
corruption of a word meaning a sea-marsh.

Louisburgh (21 *miles from Leenane and* 14 *from Westport;
Hotels:* (I.A.C., C.) M'Dermott's (small, modern); (C.) M'Girr's
(also small)) is a dull village of 400 inhabitants, within a
mile of the sea, and as free as Athenry from all attempt to
adorn itself with outward attraction. There is salmon fishing
in the rivers near for 10s. a day. Boats can be had to visit
Clare Island, to which it is the nearest point. Its only piece of
antiquity is the disused chapel, now converted to secular uses.

Between this and Westport cyclists will find pleasant going,
and the views of Croagh Patrick on the land side (page 230) and
of Clew Bay on the other make the scenery delightful. At Murrisk is the Croagh Patrick Hotel, small, though it has recently
blossomed from a mere inn into an hotel. Directly behind
it is the recognised ascent of Croagh Patrick. Near the shore,
is MURRISK ABBEY, which derives its name from the Barony.
This religious house was founded by the O'Malley family for
Austin Friars. (Entrance from north side.) The *east window*, of
the 15th century, is rather uncommon and effective. Below is
a fragmentary crucifix, and at the *stone altar* a "holed stone."
Some windows outside the north-east walls may be earlier than
the eastern one; and outside the north door of the chancel is a

chapel roofed over in the fashion of the earliest buildings, with an upper room.

Westport (*Hotels :* Railway (commercial); Bath). The only architectural feature of the place is the handsome *Protestant Church* built by the Marquis of Sligo, and the only attractions the sea-bathing and the beautiful desmesne grounds (belonging to Lord Sligo), to which the public are freely admitted.

Otherwise the town is not very attractive. In summer steamers sail from the quay for Sligo, Glasgow, and Liverpool.

Croagh Patrick mountain (2510 feet). This is popularly known as " The Reek," and is a height of unusual interest. The ascent may be made about 6 miles from Westport, opposite a bridge at the head of an inlet, close by St. Patrick's Church, Lecanvey ; or a mile farther on, at the back of the little hotel at Murrisk, itself called Croagh Patrick. As the ascent of the mountain is comparatively easy, entirely without danger except in mist, and by a clearly marked path, there is no necessity for the assistance of guides. Ponies can be taken three-fourths of the way up the mountain. Croagh Patrick is regarded as sacred to St. Patrick. While sojourning in Connaught the saint was accustomed to spend Lent on the mountain fasting and praying. There is also a tradition that he collected together on the top of the mountain all the serpents in Ireland, and drove them thence into the sea, and a hollow in the mountain is pointed out as the place in which they endeavoured in vain to take refuge on their descent.

The mountain, which is formed of quartzite, rises abruptly from the eastern margin of Clew Bay. Its cone-shaped summit, and its abrupt rise from the shore, lend to it an appearance of greater height than it actually possesses. On account of its connection with St. Patrick, it is celebrated as a place of religious pilgrimage, and at certain seasons it is climbed by pilgrims from all parts of Ireland, who " perform stations " as they ascend.

De Quincey, who as a boy of 15 climbed the mountain, in 1800, wrote home that Croagh Patrick was " the highest mountain in Ireland." At the top he found "a circular wall very rough and craggy, on which, at St. Patrick's Day, all the Papists, for many miles round, run on their knees (quite bare) till the skin is off."

A BOWLEY HOUSE, ACHILL.

The view from the summit embraces a wide stretch of country from Galway in the south to Sligo in the north, and eastwards an undefined extent of undulating ground forming the central plain of Ireland. The chief features of the prospect are Clew Bay, with its numerous islets at the western base of the mountain, and the wild and mountainous cliffs of Achill in the distance. To the south-west there is a broad moor, bounded by Mweelrea (2688 feet) and other quartzite mountains stretching between Killery Bay and Lough Mask ; beyond them are the glittering peaks of the Twelve Pins (Benbaun, the big "Ben," is probably visible exactly over Delphi), northwards are the ranges of the Ox Mountains, and adjoining Lough Conn the isolated dome of Nephin (2646 feet).

CLEW BAY, in shape, resembles the pretty bay of Port Erin in Man. It is of course several times larger and, owing to the small archipelago of islands at the east end,—"like so many dolphins and whales basking there,"—is not so clearly cut, but the rectangular form, the deep retreat, its narrowed mouth and the protection of the latter by hills at the north-west corner, all find their parallel. Its beauties are indeed far famed.

Geologists have proved the movement of the ice-flow from east to west along the bay by the discovery of marked rocks on Old Head, Louisburgh, besides the great blocks there of "Serpentine, torn from the north slopes of Croagh Patrick Ridge" (*Hull*).

Clare Island, at the mouth of the bay, has an area of 3949 acres, and its highest elevation is the Hill of Knock (1520 feet) presenting bold and precipitous cliffs to the Atlantic. The island is most conveniently visited from Achill Sound. Of the Cistercian Abbey, founded in 1224, there are remains in which may be seen some fragments of fresco paintings and the so-called tomb of Grace O'Malley. Notice the coat of arms, bearing a boar and the motto (—of the Royal Marines !). The tower of Granuaile Castle, the ancient residence of the celebrated Grace O'Malley, is situated above the harbour on the east. This lady became the leader of her clan, and eventually gained the title of "Grace of the Heroes." She was first married to O'Flaherty, Prince of Connemara, and on his decease to Sir Richard Bourke. "Tradition," says Otway, "hands down a singular item of the marriage-contract. The marriage was to last *for certain* but one year, and if at the end of that period either said to the other,

'I dismiss you,' the union was dissolved. It is said that during that year Grana took good care to put her own creatures in all M'William's eastward castles that were valuable to her, and then, one fine day, as the Lord of Mayo was coming up to the castle of Corrig-a-Howly, near Newport, Grana spied him, and cried out the dissolving words, 'I dismiss you.' We are not told how M'William took the snapping of the matrimonial chain. It is likely that he was not sorry to have a safe riddance of such a virago." Grace was invited to London by Queen Elizabeth, who tried various ways of showing her attentions ; but the wild daughter of the west could not appreciate the kindness of her entertainer.

Westport to Achill Island (26¼ *miles by train, and* 9 *on to Dugort by road*). The route embraces varied views of the mountains and of Clew Bay. At Newport, finely situated on Clew Bay, there is an hotel, and fishing on the Newport River and in the Beltra Lakes. In the neighbourhood are the ruins Burrishoole Abbey, and a beautiful glen in the heart of the mountains.

Arrived at Mallaranny, often spelt and always pronounced, Mulranny, we find the hotel (I.A.C.) of the Midland Great Western Railway ; it is connected with the station by a short path leading between hedges of rhododendron and fuchsia. Whoever had the idea of planting an hotel here had an inspiration, for the situation is perfect, one of the sweetest spots in the west. The land narrows to a neck, not a mile across, which connects the great Curraun Peninsula with the mainland. On this neck, facing Clew Bay, is the famous hotel. It stands on ground rising from the beach, and looks over a fringe of trees to the sweeping sands of its own small bay, and beyond to Croagh Patrick and the further shore. Low-lying green islets stud the foreground, and a raised causeway, built by the Company, leads across to the pier or quay. The hotel is provided with electricity from its own power-house. The green lawns (croquet and tennis) are well tended, and surrounded by a rich growth of flowering shrubs. Behind are acres of rough hilly ground belonging to the hotel, covered by heather and bramble, and traversed by paths provided with seats, while a man might walk for days on the hills beyond. The hotel is open all the year round, and as the freshness of the air is tempered by the direct action of the

Gulf Stream, the climate is far milder in winter than many places further south, as is evidenced by the wonderful growth of the rhododendron, arbutus, fuchsia, etc. It is especially to be recommended to invalids, who will find six well-built salt-water baths in the building. These are provided with water pumped straight from the sea. For those who are hardier, bathing huts are provided near the quay. Visitors at the hotel are allowed free fishing on the Owengarve River. But the great feature of the place is the really sporting golf course, which, though only nine holes, bids fair to become one of the most popular. This lies beyond the village on the east. On the west, close at hand, is the church, and at the back the little railway line winds away at the base of the precipices of the Curraun Peninsula to Achill Island, for which Mulranny is a good centre. The Railway Company gives combined rail and hotel tickets, and this enterprise of theirs deserves backing, as it has been carried out with great care and excellent design. The hotel itself is under first-rate management.

From Mulranny to Achill Sound is a matter of only 8 miles. Rail and road run side by side. Once each way in the day the Railway Company runs a rail-motor instead of a train from Westport to Achill. This goes up early in the morning but comes down from Achill at 6.20 P.M., and advantage should certainly be taken of it (cycles not carried), as it is a perfect observation-car giving wide views in all directions.

From Mulranny a road (30 miles) leads to Belmullet (*Hotels:* (C.) Erris; (C.) Sea View; Royal, (all I.A.C)), by Blacksod Bay. For the proposed development of this district see p. 205.

ACHILL.

HOTELS at DUGORT.—(I.A.C., C.) Slievemore; Strand; (C.) Mountain View; Sea View. At ACHILL SOUND there is an inn.

DISTANCES.—Achill Sound to Dugort, 9 miles. From the Sound (by rail) to Westport, 26¼ miles; Claremorris, 52¼; Sligo, 105½; Dublin, 187¼.

The island has an area of 51,521 acres, and is triangular in shape, its length from east to west being about 15 miles, and from north to south 12 miles.

The fisheries are of great value, but there is need of capital and energy to develop them, and swifter communication with the interior of Ireland. As it is, many of the inhabitants are in a chronic state of poverty, a fact sufficiently evident from a glance at the huts of rough cobbles and turf in which they dwell ; but here, as in other parts of the country, the standard of living has improved. Relief work in the shape of road-making is given in the winter. The lace industry has grown, the Carrickmacross lace-making being the staple work of many a home. There is a good deal of temporary migration to England and Scotland in seasons when agricultural labour is in demand, especially is this the case in regard to the potato crops in Dumfries, "tatie coppers," as they are called, going over in their hundreds. In Achill there are no fences and few even of the rough stone walls forming boundaries, therefore a large proportion of the time of the natives is taken up in "herding" the stock. Peat-preserving also takes up many hours of labour, as an old dame said, "It's the wan blessing we have, but what with the cutting and spreading and stacking and carrying, there's a deal of work to it!" In the height of the peat-cutting in May it is a sight to see a fleet of as many as eighty turf-laden boats go up with the flooding tide at Achill Sound.

The scenery of Achill is most beautiful, in spite of the fact of its almost treeless condition, and the heights of the near islands and the mainland seen as a background to its own rock-fringed bays or stupendous cliffs would lead even the most prosaic person to enthusiasm.

The chief town is DUGORT on the north, where are the hotels mentioned above. Mr. Sheridan who owns the Slievemore is known far and wide as one of the proprietor-hosts of Ireland. The Strand Hotel is on the beach, where there is a magnificent strand and huts for the accommodation of bathers. Seal-shooting may be had, and white and brown trout fishing off the sand-banks. Dugort is a Protestant settlement established in the famine times of '47 by not altogether unquestionable methods. The little place is growing more and more popular as a tourist resort. Long cars meet the midday trains at Achill Sound.

The highest summit on the island is Slievemore (2204 feet), the ascent of which is comparatively easy. CROAGHAUN (2192 feet) is noticeable on account of its extraordinary cliffs descending to the Atlantic, in a steep incline of 60 degrees. They are the highest marine cliffs in the world, and the home of the golden eagle. In these western hills of Achill, as at Erris Head and Belmullet, the geologist will find "archæan" rocks "consisting chiefly of gneiss with masses of schist."

To the south of Slievemore is the semicircular Keem Bay, where there is a salmon fishery. Here are picked up the Achill amethysts, much sought after and becoming rarer. Not far off was the home of the well-known Captain Boycott, now in ruins.

To see the island properly it is necessary to run right round the south end by some means or another, following the grandly named "Atlantic Drive," a very rough road, degenerating at times on the western side into a mere grass-grown mountain track, with one zigzag and precipitous descent. There is no doubt whatever that this road will soon be greatly improved and form one of the features of the island. The views from the south end looking down Achill Sound are bewilderingly beautiful. The giant Corraun peninsula near at hand, the hills of Murrisk behind, and the heights of Clare island to the west, blending in a grand panorama. The rock-fringed shore on the west recalls parts of Cornwall. From the tiny hamlet of Dooagh the famous **Meenaun Cliffs** may be visited. Dooagh is a miserable little place, with many houses tumbling in ruin, and the rest with their unmortared stone and thatch roofs weighted by stones of a poor kind. If the tide is low the cliffs may be seen by taking a longish walk on the sands, but if high the only way is to follow one of the numerous paths between the peasants' neatly cultivated holdings and breast the hill to the turf-cutting colony above — very rough walking — after this there is a stretch of slippery heather-grown upland, but neither so steep nor rough as what has preceded it; the total distance from the village is about 1½ miles. The CLIFFS are 1000 feet in height, and as they are totally unguarded, care must be taken in the approach. They are not vertical, but razor-edged and streaked with yellow and grey strata. The action of the waves has hollowed out some into the semblance of great arches known as the *Cathedral Cliffs*.

A visit should be paid, if time permit, to Inisglore and Iniskea islands, celebrated in ancient legend, and formerly the haunts of saints and recluses, of whose long-gone tenancy there is still abundant evidence in numerous crosses and the ruins of sacred edifices.

All this part of the western coast is of great interest; and from Erris Head round these cliffs of Achill and Clare island into Westport the coast abounds in fine scenery which is at present little known. Sir Harry Johnston, the great African traveller, wrote in the visitors' book at the Slievemore Hotel, in 1902, "The side view of Croaghaun cliffs I include amongst the thousand bits of choice scenery I have met in all my travels." Sir John Franklin also said, just before starting on his last fatal voyage, that the view from the summit of Croaghaun was the grandest panorama he had met with in all his travels.

ROUTE II (see page 216).

GALWAY TO CLIFDEN via LOUGH CORRIB AND RECESS.

By steamer on Lough Corrib to Cong, and thence by car viâ Clonbur and
Maam to Maam Cross, Recess, and Clifden.
For sailings of steamer between Galway and Cong, see pink pages.

Lough Corrib is about 25 miles in length, and its greatest breadth is about 8 miles. The country immediately adjoining the shores is flat and uninteresting, but the numerous rocky islets, some of them clothed with stunted trees, lend picturesqueness to the scene, while to the north-west the towering forms of the Connemara Mountains are seen in the distance to great advantage. According to fable the word Corrib is corrupted from the Giant Orbsen's name. This giant, it is said, was killed by Uliin, another giant, in a great fight at Moycullen for the sovereignty of Connaught; and it was when his grave was being dug that the waters of the lake gushed out and overspread their present surface.

About ten miles from Galway the lake contracts considerably, so as almost to give the idea of two lakes. The lower reach thus produced has very few islands upon it, but the upper expanse has so many as to have given rise to the saying that there was an island for every day of the year.

Steaming up the Corrib river we pass, on the right, 1 mile from Galway, Menlough Castle (Sir Valentine Blake) now in ruins. A little beyond this the Clare-Galway river enters the lake.

Clare-Galway is 5 miles up this stream. An account of its ruins, by Messrs. Kelly and Westropp, may be found in the *Ant. Handbook*, 1897. The

LOUGH CORRIB

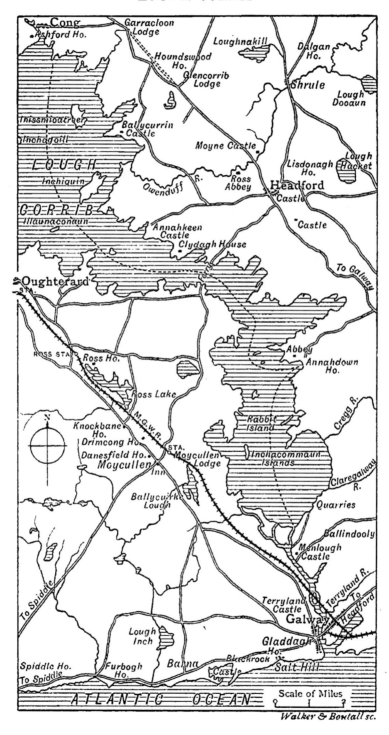

Scale of Miles

Walker & Boutall sc.

SEAL CAVES, ACHILL.

Franciscan Abbey was built in 1290 in a picturesque situation; and even after the dissolution in 1537 the faithful friars lingered round their home for two hundred years. ¢ The tower, with traceried windows, is graceful; and on the north of it is a chapel still used once a year for celebration of Mass. The *east window* of the chancel is of the same (15th century) date as the tower. The cloisters and friary buildings stood on the south side.

The *Castle* was one of the Clanricarde foundations.

At 5 miles we pass on the left the Inchacommaun islands, and shortly afterwards on our right Rabbit Island, where Lord Headley frequently camps. Further on, on the right, we see Annaghdown Castle and Abbey, both in ruins.

At Killabeg, where there is a ferry, tea can be got at a cottage ¼ mile from the pier. 3 miles off is Headford (*Hotel:* Macormack's), a clean and prosperous town, about 1 mile from which, picturesquely situated on the Owenduff, is Ross Abbey, in remarkably fine preservation, and containing a number of old monuments. To the north of the abbey is the old castle of Moyne.

After we enter the upper reaches of the lake the islands become more numerous, some of them being of considerable extent. On Inchagoil (*Inis-au-Ghoil*, the "island of the foreigner"), Lugnat, or Lugnauld, a contemporary, and believed to be a nephew of St. Patrick, took up his residence. His pillar stone, with the inscription—LIE LUGNAEDON MACC LMENUEH—is still to be seen, and near it the remains of a church supposed to have been founded by St. Patrick.

The scenery improves greatly as we get northward until, with the Connemara hills looming larger as we approach, with the many charming islets wooded to the water's edge, and finally with the fir-woods round Cong, it is well worth the journey.

Ashford House (Lord Ardilaun) is well seen as the steamer sweeps round into the little wooded bay, but not a vestige of the village appears. It is in fact about 2 miles away to the left. Cong (*Hotels:* (C) Clare Arms; Ryan's; both small but clean) has many attractions, bringing sight-seers from all over the world. The sights include the abbey, demesne grounds and caves. The **abbey** is partly situated in the grounds of Lord Ardilaun (*admission at the cottage left of the carved gateway*). The ruins received careful attention at the hands of Sir Benjamin Guinness, the father of Lord Ardilaun, who placed them under proper control and rebuilt some of the cloister arcade.

St. Féichin of Fore, who erected churches early in the **7th**
century on High Island (page 223), built here also a church.
The abbey was founded in 1129, by whom is unknown.
Afterwards, in the last part of the 12th century, King
Roderic O'Connor, the last monarch of Ireland, died, after
15 years of cloister life, within these buildings. Petrie con.
siders that most of the remaining walls date from the monk.
king's time.

After entering, follow the path till another goes back (right)
at an acute angle to the cloister. Here we have a piece of
uncommon "restoration." The arcading at the four corners
above the bases of the shafts is modern, and was designed and
erected by a local stone-mason.

Beyond are three fine EARLY DOORWAYS facing you, in the
western wall, which afford a good illustration of the transition
from Norman to Early English. That on the extreme left is
quite unlike the other two, and of simple Norman character.
The central door is of somewhat more ornate Norman ; and the
right-hand one of the three, the west door of the Refectory, has
mouldings of the Early English shape, and is much more
elaborate.

Returning to the junction of the paths, pass onward through
a small arched gateway which leads to a bridge. From this a
fine view of Ashford House can be had. At the far end of the
bridge the carved key-stone is supposed to represent King Rory.
Close by the bridge is the ancient fishing-house of the monks.

The very plain and unattractive CHURCH is entered from
the road ; a fine late Norman arch forms an entrance ; notice
its capitals. The east window, of three lancet-shaped lights,
is smothered in ivy. Beneath a grave-slab, railed over,
in the middle of the *chancel floor*, rest some of the old abbots of
this house ; and adjoining it is the reputed grave of King Rory
O'Connor, over which is a curious incised cross, without arms.
The royal recluse was really buried at Clonmacnois.

South of the chancel are some gloomy chambers, one vaulted,
of early character.

In the early part of the 19th century the parish priest found in an oaken
chest in one of the cottages of the village the celebrated *Cross of Cong*, which
is now in the Dublin Museum (page 15). It is a piece of very delicate
and beautiful metal-work, and was originally made about 1123 for the Archbishop of Tuam, and was probably brought hither by King O'Connor. It

has been studded with other precious stones besides the central crystal, and the copper face is richly adorned with interwoven tracery of gold. The whole forms a metal case for the inner cross of oak ; and an inscription states that it contains a portion of "the cross on which the founder of the world suffered" (*M. Stokes*).

In this Abbey also was kept, during the 14th century, the *Shrine of St. Patrick's Tooth*, now in the Dublin Museum.

Some very interesting *funeral customs* of great antiquity have remained in this village up to the present day. After a procession to the Abbey, a pause is made at the cross-roads, and crosses are deposited beneath an ash tree. The same ceremony is found at Bannow, and is also met with among the Pyrenees and in France.

The demesne of ASHFORD. (Ticket, obtained in village, must be presented *punctually* at 11 or 3.) The grounds, which extend for more than two miles along the borders of the lough, are finely laid out, and there are large herds of red and fallow deer. The mansion-house is an extensive pile of buildings in the castellated style, the materials being white and gray limestone. The garden and grounds only are shown.

The grounds surrounding the mansion of Lord Ardilaun are on one side bounded by a wilderness of limestone rocks. While to the south of the village the road is overhung by woods and flourishing young plantations, to the north hardly any sign of vegetation is visible, the landscape presenting an assemblage of gray limestone hills and boulders scattered about in the wildest confusion. The geologist who makes a stay at Cong will be able to collect many Upper Silurian fossils at Boocann and other places to the west of it.

Loughs Corrib and Mask are joined by a river, which for three-fourths of its course has a *subterranean stream*, and reappears again in the Mill Pond, 72 feet in depth. An attempt was made to connect the lakes by a canal, afterwards called the "great blunder," but the porous character of the limestone rendered the enterprise abortive, after enormous sums of money had been expended on it. It is indeed this characteristic of the limestone that explains the subterranean passage made by the river. At various places there are openings where the course of the stream may be seen.

The most remarkable of the caverns is the **Pigeon Hole** (Pollna-g-columb), so called from the fact that it was at one time frequented by pigeons. The Pigeon Hole may be reached through Lord Ardilaun's grounds, or by the public road, the distance from Cong being about a mile. The descent to the cavern is made by a flight of sixty steps. It is a curious sight to look upward on a sunny day and see the light glistening through the screen of foliage above. In winter, when the river is in flood, it covers the floor at the foot of the steps, so that there is no standing room beyond them. A legend states that twelve sacred trout inhabit the pool. **Captain Webb's Cave** figured in the tragic family history of that local Bluebeard.

The distance from CONG TO LEENANE is about 27 miles. For a considerable distance we skirt the shores of Lough Corrib, of which there are good views. About midway we pass Carrick House, an anglers' hotel, almost on the shore of the loch. At Maam Bridge the road to Maam Station and Recess and Clifden, etc., goes off over a bridge (left). The tiny white hotel here faces an amphitheatre of heights, the Maamturk Mountains being right opposite. The Leenane road passes between these and Joyces' country.

By a branch line from Claremorris **Ballinrobe** (*Hotel:* Valkenburg's), the nearest station to Lough Mask, can be reached.

At **Clonbur,** midway between Loughs Mask and Corrib, is (I.A.C) *Mount Gable Hotel,* a convenient place to stay for fishing, which is free. From Clonbur a road leads to Leenane (20½ miles), passing Lough Nafooey on the way.

Lough Mask, lying in a direction almost due north and south, is about 10 miles in length, and little more than 4 in breadth. Owing to the proximity of the mountains to the west, the scenery in its vicinity far surpasses that adjoining Lough Corrib. The lake contains upwards of twenty islands, the largest of which is Inishmaan, on which there are remains of a fort said to have been founded by Eoghan Beul, King of Connaught, in the beginning of the 6th century. He was killed at Sligo in 537 in battle with the people of Ulster, having previously ordered his body to be buried in an erect position "facing Ulster," with a "javelin in his hand, that even in death he might affright his enemies. The position of the body seemed to act as a charm upon the people of Connaught, who subsequently won every battle, until the people of the north of Ireland came with a numerous host, and carried the body northwards across the river Sligo. It was buried at the other side at Aenagh Locha Gile, with the mouth down, that it might not be the means of causing them to fly before the Connacians." The remains of a small but beautiful abbey also exist on the island.

The ruins of Mask Castle, a fortress built by the English in 1238, are on the shore opposite the island. Near it was one of the residences of *Captain Boycott*, well known some years ago in connection with the agrarian disturbances. On an island not far from Ballinrobe are the ruins of a castle of the O'Connors, known as Hag's Castle. It is surrounded by a circular enclosure, and the island on which it stands is said to be artificial.

WESTPORT BY RAIL FROM ATHLONE.

The route from Dublin to Athlone is included in that from Dublin to Galway (page 177). Should Athlone be reached by the Great South-Western Railway, it will be necessary to take a car for the Midland Great Western Station on the Roscommon side of the river. From Athlone to Westport our journey for some distance adjoins the western shores of Lough Ree.

The first town we pass of special interest is **Roscommon, 18** miles (*Hotels:* The Royal; (C.) Grealy's; both small). Its ruins are of important interest for the antiquarian, who will find useful notes on Roscommon and Ballintubber in the *Ant. Handbook* for 1897. The town derives its name from an abbey founded in the 8th century by St. Coman or Comanus.

About the middle of the 13th century a DOMINICAN PRIORY was also founded by Feidlim O'Connor, King of Connaught, who was interred within its walls, and whose tomb, with mutilated effigy, is still pointed out. It is a very mixed work of art, in fine Irish marble. The monument represents a mailed recumbent figure placed upon an altar-tomb, the sides ornamented with several compartments, in each of which stands a figure mailed and armed. The monument has, however, undergone severe mutilation.

The CASTLE, visible from the railway station, about a quarter of a mile to the north of the town, was built in 1269, when the office of Justiciary of Ireland was held by Robert D'Ufford. There is, however, no doubt that a fortress of a much earlier date previously occupied the site. The walls, of great thickness, are defended at intervals by large semicircular towers. The building is now a total ruin, although it is said that portions were habitable at the period of the Civil War, when they were set on fire by a party retreating after the battle of Aghrim. "The work of destruction must have been done by gunpowder, as large masses of masonry lie close by."

Four miles from *Castlerea* is the Edwardian Castle of Ballintober.

Ballyhaunis (43¾ miles) is the best station from which to visit the church of Knock (8 miles by hired car), where the miracles of healing and supernatural visions attracted large crowds of pilgrims some years ago. Crutches and other relics may be seen at the church, which is still visited by many devout Roman Catholics.

At **Claremorris** (46¾ miles) (several small hotels) is an important junction, whence a line goes north to Sligo and south to Tuam, see page 205. For Cong take rail to Ballinrobe, and hence it is 7 miles by road.

At **Manulla** (47¾ miles) a branch line turns northwards to Ballina (20¼ miles). The next station, 52 miles from Athlone, is

Castlebar (*Hotels :* (I.A.C., C.) Imperial ; Read's), the county town. Station about 1 mile from the town. In the rebellion of 1798 Castlebar gained notoriety from an engagement between a small French force and a party of English soldiers. The contending parties were nearly equal in number, being about 1000 strong each. The English were but badly provided with ammunition, and, with the exception of a party of the Fraser Fencibles, were raw militia. The encounter is yet facetiously alluded to as the "Castlebar Races." A slab to the memory of the Fraser Highlanders who fell in the action was erected in the church by Colonel Fraser.

In Castlebar was executed in 1786 the notorious George Robert Fitzgerald, better known as "Fighting Fitzgerald." His residence was at Turlough, about 4 miles east of Castlebar, where his remains rest among some ruins in the demesne, overlooked by an ancient round tower. From the railway we obtain a good view of Croagh Patrick before reaching Westport (p. 230).

For the routes from Westport (1) to Leenane and Clifden see page 223 (reverse way) ; (2) to Achill, page 232.

WESTPORT TO SLIGO

AND THENCE TO DUBLIN.

To Ballina by rail *viâ* Manulla Junction. From Ballina by mail-car to Sligo
viâ Dromore. From Sligo to Dublin *viâ* Boyle, Carrick-on-Shannon, and
Longford.
(The direct route from Westport by rail to Sligo is *viâ* Claremorris.)

	Miles.		Miles.
WESTPORT.		Killala round tower and	
CASTLEBAR . . .	11	cathedral, 8 m. *l*.]	
MANULLA JUNCTION . .	15	Ox Mountains (*r*)	
FOXFORD	26½	DROMORE, WEST . . .	51
Lough Conn.		Aughris Head (*l*)	
Nephin.		Ballysodare Bay (*l*)	
		BALLYSODARE	67½
BALLINA	35¾	Rapids.	
Killala Bay.		Abbey.	
[Roserk Abbey, 4 m. *l*.		Knocknarea (*l*).	
Moyne Abbey, 6 m. *l*.		SLIGO	72¾

All tourists who have come as far as this point on the western
coast are strongly recommended to see the best bit of the Sligo
district, if time allows. The route between Westport and Castlebar will be found described at page 241.

The first station after Manulla is *Foxford* (*Hotel:* Coghlan's),
on Lough Cullin, where, as on the Moy, there is excellent
fishing. Loughs Cullin and Conn are joined by a narrow strait,
crossed by a pontoon bridge. Leaving Foxford, a fine view is
obtained of Lough Conn, a large sheet of water, being nearly
9 miles in length by about 1 to 3 in width. On the west side of
it rises the great Nephin Mountain, with a finely-shaped conical
summit, 2646 feet above the sea-level. It is a singular fact
that there is occasionally a reverse flow of the Lower Lake,
usually called Lough Cullin, into the upper, or Lough Conn
proper. The lake is situated about 40 feet above the sea, and
can have no tide communication with it. The banks are in many
parts of fine sand, which indicates the high-water line. The
shores of the Lower Lake, on the west side, abound in little bays
and creeks, and show some bold outlines.

Ballina (pron. *Bal-e-nár;* *Hotels:* (C.) Imperial; Central;
(I.A.C.) Moy; all commercial. *For cars see pink pages*).

Ballina has rather a picturesque entrance, for near the station is a long row of one-story, thatched cottages, adorned with all shades of colour-wash. Corrugated iron is unfortunately superseding thatch. The town itself is uninteresting, but has the advantage of some better shops than are usually found in an Irish town of this size. It has also a fine salmon river, two good stone bridges, a modern Roman Catholic Cathedral and a college, the latter a conspicuous object from the railway on the way to Killala. The Moy Fishery Company owns the fishing in the tidal water, but angling in the fresh water above the town is good, and tickets can be got at 7s. 6d. and 10s. a day from Mr. J. C. Wilson, Ballina.

There is salmon and trout fishing on LOCH CONN (several hotels at Crossmolina), about 6 miles from Ballina. The bay is famous as the rendezvous of the French invaders in 1798. The garrison of Killala, only forty men, was surprised by the French general, Humbert, who landed with a thousand men. Next day a detachment of the French were driven in by an English piquet, who, advancing too far, were ambuscaded, and suffered considerable loss. Towards night the French advancing, entered Ballina, and drove out the loyalists, who retreated to Foxford. The enemy retained possession for three weeks, when they were attacked by General Trench, and ultimately driven back to their ships.

BALLINA TO DOWNPATRICK HEAD.

From Ballina the railway runs 7 miles north-west to Killala, on Killala Bay.

ROSERK ABBEY is about 5 miles north of Ballina by the road running near the river, beautifully situated on the river Moy, and surrounded by undulating hills. This abbey is in a more perfect condition than that of Clare-Galway (page 236), which it somewhat resembles. Two miles from this are the remains of MOYNE ABBEY, built by De Bourgo in the 15th century. It flourished for about 150 years, was a renowned seat of learning, and boasted the best and most extensive library in any of the western monasteries. Even in its decay some of the ancient glories are still perceptible. North of it are the ruins of the first Christian Church of the time of St. Patrick. The road running past these interesting sights is not the direct one between Ballina and Killala, but is to it as a bow to its string. Killala (small *hotel*) played a part in the disturbances of 1798. The principal object of interest is the very fine and complete Round Tower which rises from the midst of the houses. The bishop's palace forms part of the workhouse. In the immediate neighbourhood of the town is the hill where the ancient princes of Inerughy and Tyrawley were crowned. Northwest from this a road of 10 miles leads to *Ballycastle* (*Hotel*), from which can be reached

Downpatrick Head, 9 miles north of Killala, a succession of magnificent cliffs, well worthy of a visit. In ascending the Head visitors are startled by coming suddenly on a great chasm, caused by the surface of the hill having fallen in. Cautiously approaching this abyss, and looking down, the ocean is seen rolling in at a depth of 2000 feet, through a subterranean passage called the Poulashantana.

The journey from **Ballina** to **Sligo** is 37 miles, and it is possible to go by car once a day, changing at Dromore. Fare 5s. 6d. The cycling is fair generally. From Ballina to Dromore the road is, generally speaking, unattractive. The country is flat moorland, and only relieved by the distant view, on the right, of the Ox Mountains. Beyond Dromore (*large inn*) the aspect of the country is more cheerful, being better cultivated and more fertile, though to the right it is still mountainous. On the left is Aughris Head, a promontory guarding the southern shore of Sligo Bay. Before reaching Ballysodare we have a view on the left of the lake-like bay of the same name.

Ballysodare, finely placed at the foot of the Lurgan Hills, is a village on the Owenmore, which falls into the bay over a series of rocky ledges, forming a succession of rapids, ending with a fine though small *waterfall*. The Abbey of St. Féichin overlooks the rapids on the west side of the river, where the only good view of them is to be obtained. The remarkable salmon ladders farther up should be seen. The place is much decayed, and little more than a wreck of its former condition.

Here the road turns northward, in full view of Knocknarea, on the left, with a southern face that is a very cataract of ochre-coloured screes.

A little south of Ballysodare is **Collooney** Junction (p. 205), already mentioned in connection with the projected railway line from Belmullet, which will form part of the "All-Red Route."

SLIGO.

RAILWAY STATION.—(Midland Great Western Railway).

HOTELS.—(I. A. C., C.) *Victoria*, good, English Style ; *Imperial.*

DISTANCES.—Ballina, 37 miles ; Ballysodare, 5 ; Ballyshannon, 27 ; Belleek, 32 ; Bundoran, 22½ ; Dromore, west, 23 ; Enniskillen (*rail*), 49 ; Glencar (round), 20 ; Grange, 9 ; Lough Gill (round), 23 ; Manor Hamilton, 15.

Steamers leave Sligo for *Glasgow* (Laird) twice a week ; for *Liverpool* (Sligo Company) once a week, and for *Westport* once a fortnight ; for *Belmullet* see *pink pages.*

Pop. 11,163.

Sligo is one of the most prosperous-looking places in Ireland. It is built on both sides of the River Garavogue. Its streets are not only well built, but they are well brushed ; there are good shops, and also some fine public buildings, including the Town Hall, the Court House, and a wonderful stone National School covered with rose-trees. There are two bridges near together and at right angles to one another owing to the bend in the river, and the abbey and cathedral mentioned below are worth a visit.

The town and its pleasant surroundings deserve to be better known than they are, especially as there are numerous excursions to be made, some of them being of quite unusual interest ; the scenery of Loughs Gill and Glencar is charming, and should certainly be seen by every tourist in western Ireland. For those again with antiquarian tastes, it is a land of plenty, as there are many ruins and prehistoric remains in the district. (See *Journal of R. S. Ant. Ireland*, 1896).

The history of Sligo begins with legend. When "Nuada of the Silver Hand" vanquished and killed the king of the Firbolgs, the royal corpse was buried in the Sligo strand, and it is fabled that "the tide will never cover it." Among recorded facts is the founding of the Monastery and Castle by Fitzgerald, Earl of Kildare, in the 13th century. In the civil wars the town was captured by the Parliamentary troops under Coote.

The chief lion of the town is the **Abbey of Sligo**, founded about 1252 by Maurice Fitzgerald, Lord Justice, now a fine ruin. It was consumed by fire in 1414, but soon afterwards was re-erected. The choir has a beautiful east window, of "reticulated" tracery, still perfect ; the slender ringed shafts are a good feature. Under this is a very rare specimen of a stone altar ;

the quaint figure of St. Dominic on the top is the most interesting feature. The tomb near is said to be that of King Conor.
Near the obstructive central wall is the O'Crean monument
beneath a once beautiful canopy.

The almost perfect miniature cloisters are well worth exam-
ining. One of them is carved in a design representing Irish
lace ; in the corner near it will be found a true lover's knot on
a boss.

In another part of the town are St. John's Church, a fine
stone building with an uncommon east window, and the modern
Roman Catholic Cathedral. The splendid carillon of chimes of
the CATHEDRAL will have been heard before reaching it. This
is one of the most important modern buildings in Ireland, and
Romanesque in character—a style uncommon in recent work.
(Notice, in passing, the well-carved statue of St. Patrick on the
wall of an outer building.) The tower containing the chimes is
massive ; and the winged angel over the east apse is a remarkable symbolic figure—not of Peace. Owing to the lack of carved
ornament within, the bare forms of this style are unrelieved,
and the whole effect, though dignified, is heavy. The most
striking feature is the wide and lofty triforium.

Among other advantages of the neighbourhood, there is good
sea-bathing, with accommodation, at Rosses Point, 4 or 5 miles
away, and also a capital 18-hole golf course with a club-house.

The principal excursion from Sligo is that to **Lough Gill** or
Gilly, as it is sometimes called. This may be done by row-boat
(hire 5s. to head of lough) ; or, in summer by motor-boat leaving
Sligo daily at 3 P.M., charge 1s. 6d. This goes to Dromohair,
and allows 2 hours there before return. The round of the
lough may be made by road. In this case it is best to start on
the north side. After leaving the town in a direct line with the
Victoria Bridge, keep to the right at all turns after the first.
The first leads to the desmesne of *Hazlewood* situated at the
north-west end of the lough. Permission may sometimes be
obtained to pass through it. The main road is good, but for $3\frac{1}{2}$
miles nothing is seen of the lough, until, on climbing a hill, it
is discovered lying below. Its many islands and sloping,
wooded shores give it a resemblance to Killarney. The first
object of interest on the north shore is *Breffny Castle*, near
which is the *Fern Glen*, which should be explored if time
allows. Then pass on through O'Rourke's "smiling valley" to

Dromohair. This means a detour from the lake, as there is no road close to the south side for some miles. At **Dromohair** (*Hotel* : (I.A.C., C.) *Abbey*), there are *O'Rourke's Castle*, with walls of prodigious thickness, and *St. Munchin's Abbey* to be seen. From here the road wends back to the lough through a gorge, and on reaching it careful watch should be kept for a path on the right, leading through the woods to the *Dooney Rock*, whence the most beautiful view of the lough is obtained. The richly wooded isles and headlands, the luxuriant masses of beech and oak, give a character all its own to this charming scene. Not far from this, near a school, there is to be found the most interesting sight of all, *Tober N'Alt*, a Druid altar, older than history, on which undoubtedly at one time human sacrifices were offered. The ferns growing out of the rock recesses, the constant flow of ice-cold water in the well, and the mysterious depths all add to a weird and almost uncanny scene of beauty and fascination. Total distance for the round and back to Sligo, 23 miles. As to *fishing*, salmon, trout, and pike are plentiful in the lough, and permission may be obtained by anglers from the landlord of the Victoria Hotel.

The fishing on the other Sligo beauty spot, *Glencar*, is subject to more restriction. Application as above, when terms can be ascertained.

Glencar ("the glen of the pillar-stone"), is 8 miles from Sligo, smaller, and not so beautiful as Lough Gill, but it makes a delightful round nevertheless. On the north side is Mrs. Siberry's tea-house, of a kind unique in Ireland. Mrs. Siberry, who is known far and wide, is an adept at home-made bread, scones, and sponge cakes, baked in a "pot-oven." Her milk and cream are in keeping, and let no one think they have "done" the neighbourhood of Sligo until they have had tea here. While those who want to live the "simple life," in its most attractive form, will do well to secure accommodation, which is very limited, long beforehand.

From the cottage a short rise leads to

GLENCAR WATERFALL, a good and deservedly popular pic-nickers' haunt. As you ascend the steep "brae" to this, look back at the striking views, westward, of the rocky buttresses of King's mountain, Benbulbin's southern foot. The waterfall is, to be exact, composed of three cascades, each separated by a few minutes' climb among rocks and foliage. Westward from the cottage, along the road, is the county-boundary bridge ; and here, when the wind blows from a certain point, the water of the *Struth-an-ail-an-erd* stream is driven upwards and back again over the mountain. Another path behind the cottage leads to the "Swiss Valley." Among these northern rocks fern-collectors may find some uncommon specimens, which for obvious reasons we forbear to name.

The excursion to **Knocknarea** is an enjoyable one, and may include a coast drive, a mountain ascent, and a visit to rare prehistoric remains. The whole round is about 13 miles. By taking the southern road you reach, in 3 miles, the great group of ancient cromlechs and stone monuments at CARROWMORE. A few miles north-west is a remarkable fern glen on the south side of the mountain, and from the school near this *Knocknarea,* "the Hill of Executions" (1078 feet), can be ascended. On the top of the hill is an immense cairn called Misgoun Meave, said to have been erected in honour of Queen Meave, the "Mab" of Shakespeare, Scott, and Ben Jonson ; who buried three husbands ere she herself departed. The heap of stones over her grave is 200 yards in circumference. Tradition has buried her namesake at Tara (see *Dublin Sect.* p. 45). The fine view extends from Slieve League (north-west) to Nephin (south-west).

At Lissadel House, Sir Josslyn Gore-Booth's place, north of Drumcliff Bay are the most wonderful bulb farms in the kingdom, and also Alpine gardens, freely shown to visitors. In the deer-park, north of Lough Gill, is a collection of ancient stones, sometimes called the Irish Stone-henge, but this is rather out of the way, and could not be seen very well during the run round the lake described above.

The ROAD TO BUNDORAN (the only driving connection is the mail-car which starts at 6 A.M. and has a seat for one passenger) runs northwards round the western foot of Benbulbin, and passes, in 11 miles, through **Grange**, the best boat-landing for Inismurray.

SLIGO TO LONGFORD.

The journey from Sligo to Longford by rail lies through Ballysodare to Collooney. On the left, beyond Collooney, a prominent object in which is the steeple of the handsome Roman Catholic church, we pass the demesne of Markree, the seat of Captain Bryan Cooper, with a fine castellated mansion and observatory.   Road and rail are separated between Boyle and Collooney ; for some distance beside the road Lough Arrow extends on the left, a pleasant expanse of water, about 4 or 5 miles long by 1½ wide, containing several beautiful islands, and in the same direction is Carrokee Hill (1062 feet).

Ballinafad is a small town, with a dismantled castle of the same name, founded by one of the M'Donoughs.   In its neighbourhood are two places, one entitled *Moy Tuiridh*, remarkable as the scene of a decisive battle between the ancient Belgic and Danish colonists of Ireland, and the other, *Ceis Corran*, famous in romantic legend.   The railway now rises through the Curlew Hills.

Boyle (*Hotels :* Royal ; Rockingham Arms) is well situated on the banks of the Boyle river, and exhibits an aspect of thrift and comfort.   The handsome Roman Catholic cathedral, erected 1882, occupies a prominent position to the east of the town.   The barrack was formerly the residence of the family of King-Harman, the proprietors of the town, who granted the inhabitants a small park.   Boyle is the best centre from which to fish Loughs Arrow, Gara, and Key.

The ABBEY of Boyle, on the river (north), is of a Cistercian foundation, built between 1150 and 1200.   It is of considerable interest owing to the various periods of early architecture it exhibits, the good condition of the church, the kitchen and other outbuildings, and the unusual elaboration of some of the carvings.   Of the *Church* the oldest part is the south side of the Nave, pierced by Norman arches ; opposite are Early Pointed arches of the same character as the chancel arch ; it has a large central tower.   About 2 miles away (north-east) is Lough Key.

Lough Key is a small lake, but excels many of greater extent in this district in the woods which adorn its banks.   There are several islands, the most notable being Trinity Island, with the ruins of a religious house ; and Castle Island, with a castle of the M'Diarmids, the walls of which are still standing.   Skirting the lake, and almost surrounding it, is Rockingham, the beautiful demesne of Stafford King-Harman.   There is good

Broad Haven
Benwee Head
Kid I.
Erris Hd.
Eagle I.
Carrowteige
Raheen
Doonfeeny
Glencolry
Ballyglass
Inver
Annagh Hd.
Inishglora
Inishkeeragh
Binghamstown
Glenamoy
Sl. Fyough
Carrowmore
Bangor
Elly Har.
Inishkea
N.
S.
Fallmore
Duvilaun More I.
Black Rock
Blacksod Bay
Doogort
Tullaghan B.
Saddle Hd.
Sl. More
Croghan
Achill Head
Dooaglia
ACHILL
ISLAND
Annagh I.
Moyteoge Hd.
Keel B.
Dooega Hd.
Camport B.
Bills Rocks
Achillbeg I.
CURRAUN
PENINA
Mulranny
Knocknatinnree
Nephin Beg
Nephin Beg Mts
Nephin
Bereen curragh
Buckoogh
L. Feeagh
Beltra L.
Newport
Newport B.
Illanmore
Islandeady
Dahybaun L.
R. Deel
R. Owenmore
Ballacorick Br.
Sl. Car
Owen Inny R.
CLEW BAY
Clare I.
L. Ho.
Kinnacorra Hd.
Westport B.
Westport
Old Head
Emlagh Pt.
Louisburgh
Croagh Patrick
The Triangle
Caher I.
L. Roonah
Inishturk
Runlough Pt.
Inishdalla
Ben Bury
Mines
L. Doo
Muilrea
Delphi
Killary Harb.
Inishbofin
Davillaun
Crump I.
Inishshark
Shark Hd.
Inishgort
Bofin Harb.
Ballynakill Harb.
Tullymore
Cleggan
L. Muck
L. Fee
Leenane
L. Nafooey
Devils mother
JOYCES COUNTRY
L. Kylemore
Letterfrack
High I.
Crugh I.
Omey I.
Streamstown
Benbaun
The Twelve Pins of Bunnabeola
Maam
Ebor Hall
Clifden
Ardbear B.
Derryclare L.
Maumturk Mts
Mannin Bay
Ballynahinch
L. Ardderry
L. Bofin
Inishduggn
CONNEMARA
Cashel
L. Shindilla
Slyne Head
Ballinaleama B.
Bunowen B.
Roundstone
Bertraghboy B.
JARCON

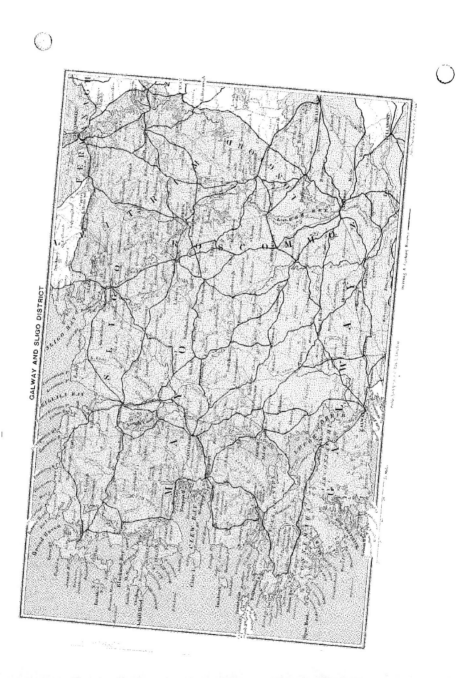

GALWAY AND SLIGO DISTRICT

trout and pike fishing, while the lake is covered with wildfowl, cormorants building their nests in the trees—a very unusual feature.

The next lough north-east of this is *Meelagh,* near which is the cemetery of Kilronan. Here was buried the famous Carolan, one of the last of the veritable Irish bards.

At **Carrick-on-Shannon** (*Hotel:* The Bush) we enter the county of Leitrim, of which it is the assize town. It was incorporated by James I. The court-house is a good building with a Doric front.

Drumsna is a pleasant little village near the well-planted estate of Mount Campbell, the residence of the late Admiral Rowley. Through a poorly cultivated country, improved by many mansions and woods, we proceed to Dromod, where interesting views are obtained of the Loughs Bofin and Boderg, both enlarge-ments of the great river Shannon.

Rooskey Bridge is an insignificant village, where the Shannon is crossed, below Lough Boderg. On our way thence we pass through Newton Forbes, and on the right, Castle Forbes, the beautiful seat of the Earl of Granard, and proceeding over a flat rich country, soon arrive at Longford.

Longford (*Hotel:* Longford Arms) possesses a fine Roman Catholic cathedral and some remains of an old castle and a Dominican abbey.

Nine miles farther on we pass Edgeworthstown, the home of Maria Edgeworth. Miss Edgeworth, one of the greatest of Ireland's literary children, was born at her grandfather's house at Black Bourton, near Oxford, but though she thus failed to own Ireland as her birthplace, her family had been associated with it for many generations, and the family place at Edge-worthstown was retained through all vicissitudes. She went to live there on her father's second marriage, which occurred only a few months after the death of her own mother. Mr. Edge-worth indeed married quickly and married often ; when the second wife died he persuaded her sister to be his wife within the year in spite of the Deceased Wife's Sister prohibition, and on her death it was not six months before he married again. Maria seems to have got on well with her numerous stepmothers, and the large family of growing sons and daughters were left largely in her charge. She educated her young step-brothers and sisters, and it was for them she began writing stories, her immensely popular *Parent's Assistant* thus originating. The household was still further increased by the addition of two of the second and third Mrs. Edgeworth's sisters, but in the never-ending turmoil and lack of privacy Maria wrote without difficulty. It was she who managed the property for her father and received the rents, and after a short interregnum she did the same for her step-brother Lovell, who succeeded him. It was at this time Sir Walter Scott paid his memorable visit. "Mrs. Edgeworth's brother," says Lockhart, "had his classic mansion filled every evening with a succession of distinguished friends" to meet the poet. Edgeworthstown was Miss Edgeworth's home during the whole of her long life, and here she died at the age of eighty-two. From the first she depicted life as she saw it, which was the secret of her great success, and those who know her works will recognise many a homely picture in their visit to this district.

Then after Cavan Junction, where a branch diverges to Cavan, we reach Mullingar, already described (p. 178).

INDEX

The first of several references is the most important.
Numbers of pages on *left* refer to the maps.

253

Printed by R. & R. CLARK, LIMITED, *Edinburgh.*

ARISAIG—**ARISAIG HOTEL.**

RECENTLY rebuilt, with modern Sanitation, and furnished as a First-Class Hotel, including a good Billiard Room. Close to the Beach. Arisaig is beautifully wooded, and is one of the healthiest and most lovely districts in the Highlands. Pleasure drives, train and steamboat excursions, and nice walks. Golf Course ½-mile from Hotel. Boating and Sea Fishing. Post and Telegraph Office near. Boots meets all trains. **Malcolm MacLure,** *Lessee.*

ISLE OF ARRAN.
CORRIE HOTEL.

BEAUTIFULLY situated close by sea, and nearest Hotel to the famous Glen Sannox. Best centre for climbing the Arras Peaks. Good Sea Fishing. Boating and Bathing. Golf and Billiards.

For Terms, etc., apply to

R. W. FORSYTH, Proprietor.

Telegrams: "**Hotel, Corrie.**"

BALLOCH—FOOT OF LOCH LOMOND.
TULLICHEWAN HOTEL.

THIS HOTEL is picturesquely situated in its own extensive pleasure grounds. It is close to Balloch Station and Pier, and occupies the most central position in the West of Scotland for Day Excursions to LOCH LOMOND, the TROSSACHS, and the CLYDE WATERING PLACES.

GARAGE, FISHING, BOATING, GOLFING, TENNIS.

BANAVIE.
LOCHIEL ARMS HOTEL.

Junction of Caledonian Canal Steamers and West Highland Railway.
ENTIRELY RECONSTRUCTED.   LICHTED BY ELECTRICITY THROUGHOUT.
"From BANAVIE, the Views of our exalted friend Ben Nevis are magnificent. The Banavie Hotel is excellent; the house is up-to-date in every respect; the service is excellent. So to travellers by this route I say, 'Put in here—the BANAVIE.' *C'est mon avis.*"—Sir F. C. BURNAND in *Punch*, 26th September 1900. **Fine New Seaside Golf Course.**
FINEST RESIDENTIAL HOTEL IN WEST HIGHLANDS.
Special Boarding Terms for Families.   Motor Bus Meets Trains and Steamers at Fort-William.   Large Garage, I.P.   Petrol and Oils Stocked.
For Terms apply Proprietor.
☞ **CAUTION**—*BEN NEVIS CAN BE SEEN FROM BANAVIE ONLY.*

BARMOUTH, N. WALES.
The Riviera of the United Kingdom.   Summer and Winter Residence.

THE CORS-Y-GEDOL HOTEL, THE MARINE HOTEL,
ST. ANN'S MANSIONS (Private Boarding House).

All facing the sea with a south-west aspect.
Specially reduced charges for the Winter Months, October to June inclusive.
GOLF LINKS.   TARIFF ON APPLICATION.
P.O. Telephone—No. 2.

BUNDORAN, IRELAND.

THE CENTRAL HOTEL
(Late SWEENY'S).

THIS Hotel is beautifully situated, overlooking the sea, and combines all the requirements of a First-Class Hotel, having been enlarged, refurnished, and lighted by Electricity throughout.

Excellent Cuisine and Wines.   Moderate Charges.   Free Salmon and Trout Fishing.   Golf Links 2 minutes' walk from Hotel.

TOM GORMAN, Proprietor.   **Telegrams: CENTRAL HOTEL, Bundoran.**

BUSHEY, HERTS.   (16 miles from Euston.)

THE HALL.

MAGNIFICENT COUNTRY MANSION HOTEL.
100 Rooms.

CHARMING Summer and Winter Country Residence.   By Day or Week. First-class fully licensed Hotel standing in beautiful park of 120 acres.

Fine Golf Links (18 holes) in Park facing the Hotel.

Turkish Baths, Swimming and ordinary baths FREE.

Tennis, Croquet, and Putting Green.
For illustrated Tariff apply—H. G. A. THIMM.
Telegrams: "Welcome, Watford."   **Telephone: 17 Watford.**

"A most pleasant and acceptable holiday souvenir."—*Buxton Advertiser.*

THE PEAK COUNTRY. By J. E. MORRIS.

Containing 12 Full-Page Illustrations in Colour.
Large Square Demy 8vo.   Bound in cloth with picture in colour on the cover.
Price 1s. 6d. net (by post 1s. 10d.).

"It is an altogether charming book, well written and splendidly illustrated."—*Belper News.*

"The book is from the pen of an interesting and clever writer, who deals with all the beauties of Peakland with fine picturesque and vivid descriptive powers."—*Buxton Herald.*

PUBLISHED BY A. & C. BLACK, LTD., 4, 5, AND 6, SOHO SQUARE, LONDON, W.
And obtainable of all Booksellers.

COLWYN BAY, N.W.

IMPERIAL (STATION) HOTEL.

FIRST CLASS. NEAR THE SEA AND PROMENADE.

HANDSOME Public Rooms and Lounges. Private Suites for Families, at Special Terms. Boarding terms.

TARIFF MODERATE.   GARAGE.   GOLF NEAR.

"Poli-Tiko-Economic" Department now open.

Telephone, 182.   Telegrams, "Imperial, Colwyn Bay."

COLWYN (NORTH WALES).

D. MAC. NICOLL, F.S.I.,

Estate Agent, etc.,

Cefn Building Estate Office, OLD COLWYN.

LAND sold in Plots or let on Building Leases, etc. Old Colwyn enjoys unrivalled view of sea and mountains; immunity from the east winds owing to Penmaen Head, and a dryness and warmth by situation on Limestone. Excellent Sea Bathing. Delightful Golf Links. Choice of rural walks almost unsurpassed on the Coast.

LEENANE HOTEL

COUNTY GALWAY.

Ideal Place for a Month's Holiday.

EXCELLENT SPORTING HOTEL AT LEENANE, CONNEMARA.

SHOOTING. Fishing on Sea and Lakes. Delightful Daily Excursions. Excellent Facilities for Bathing. Tennis and Croquet. Good Roads for Motoring. Magnificent Scenery. Motor Cars and Horse Conveyances. Garage.

Motor Coaches from Westport and Clifden stop at this Hotel.

MODERATE TARIFF.

Apply R. HENRY McKEOWN, *Proprietor.*

DORNOCH—SUTHERLAND.

GOLF.   GOLF.   GOLF.

THE SUTHERLAND ARMS HOTEL,

Adjoining the celebrated Golf Links. Two 18-hole Courses. Salmon and Sea-Trout Fishing *free* to Residents in Hotel. *En pension* terms from 10s. per day.

GARAGE.   MOTOR CARS.   POSTING.

WM. FRASER, *Proprietor.*

EASDALE—ON ROYAL ROUTE.

INSHAIG PARK HOTEL.

Situated amidst Beautiful Coastal Scenery.
Steamers call.

SEA & TROUT FISHING FREE TO VISITORS. BOATING. BATHING.

Golf at Oban 16 miles.   Garage with Pit.   Posting.

Special charges for Boarding. ✳   J. GILLIES, *Proprietrix.*

EDINBURGH.

DARLING'S REGENT HOTEL,

21 WATERLOO PLACE.

FIRST-CLASS TEMPERANCE HOTEL.

Under personal management of Miss DARLING.

Address for Telegrams—
"*Darling's Hotel,*
Edinburgh."

Telephone: 2928 Central.

EDINBURGH.

WEST END BOARDING ESTABLISHMENT

59 MANOR PLACE.

(NEAR TRAMWAYS AND RAILWAY STATIONS.)

Telegrams and Telephone } 7268 Edinburgh.   Miss SLIGHT.

FOWEY (CORNWALL).

ST. CATHERINE'S HOUSE
(PRIVATE HOTEL).

Dining, Drawing, Smoking, and Private Sitting Rooms.   Thirty Bedrooms.
Unrivalled Situation.   Facing Harbour and Channel.

**HIGHLY RECOMMENDED AS A HEALTH RESORT.   GOLF LINKS WITHIN
10 MINUTES' WALK.   MOTOR CAR KEPT.   TERMS MODERATE.**

Telephone No. 4.
Telegrams: "BROKENSHAW, FOWEY."   MRS. BROKENSHAW, *Proprietress.*

GLASGOW.

CRANSTON'S WAVERLEY TEMPERANCE HOTEL
172 SAUCHIEHALL STREET.

CAUTION.—Please see that you are taken to Cranston's Waverley, Sauchiehall Street.

Telegraphic Address: Waverley Hotel.   Telephones: 128 Douglas and 1434 Douglas.
BREAKFAST or TEA, 1/3, 1/6, 2/-; BEDROOM, with attendance inclusive, 3/-.

Stockrooms just added, from 3/- per day.   Passenger Elevator.

Other Addresses: Edinburgh, Old Waverley, Princes Street;
Edinburgh, New Waverley, Waterloo Place.

One of the most up-to-date, comfortable, and
best situated Hotels in the City.

Spacious Ladies' Drawing-room.

ELECTRIC LIGHT
THROUGHOUT.

HOTEL BALMORAL,
SAUCHIEHALL STREET, GLASGOW.

70 ROOMS.
THREE TELEPHONES.
Wires: "HOTEL BALMORAL."

CENTRAL FOR BUSINESS OR PLEASURE.

Bedroom, 3 Course Breakfast and Bath, **5/-**

2

HUNTER'S QUAY.

ROYAL MARINE HOTEL,

FIRTH OF CLYDE.

Headquarters of the Royal Clyde Yacht Club.

A FIRST-CLASS FAMILY HOTEL.

WITHIN about one hour's journey from Glasgow by Rail and Steamer, *via* Caledonian, North British, or Glasgow and South-Western Railway Coast Routes. There is a good service of Steamers to Hunter's Quay during the season, and to Kirn, three-quarters of a mile from Hotel, all the year round.

HOT and COLD, FRESH and SEA WATER BATHS, SPRAYS, DOUCHE, &c.

Golf, Bowling, Tennis, Garage.

Telegraph and Post Office within the Grounds.

Telegraphic Address—   *Telephone—*
"Hotel, Hunter's Quay."   No. 25, KIRN.

ROBERT STUART, *Manager.*

ILFRACOMBE.

LEWIS' CRESCENT BOARDING ESTABLISHMENT.

A FIRST-CLASS PENSION in unrivalled position. 3 minutes from Sea and Promenade. Large Public Rooms, Balconies, and Lounges. 54 well-appointed Bedrooms. Liberal Table. Comfortable and Homelike. Moderate and Inclusive Terms. Highly recommended.

Apply Proprietors for Tariff.

Telegrams—"Crescent Hotel."   Telephone—No. 72.

ILFRACOMBE.

BELGRAVE HOTEL.

(Fully Licensed.)

THIS Highly Recommended Hotel is centrally situated on sea-level. Spacious, well-appointed rooms fitted with every modern convenience, including Electric Light throughout.

TABLE D'HOTE (Separate Tables).   **TERMS MODERATE.**

Illustrated Tariff on application to Proprietress.

"IN ROMANTIC BADENOCH."

KINGUSSIE.
DUKE OF GORDON HOTEL.

SITUATED among the Finest Scenery of the Cairngorm Mountains. Entirely rebuilt
and renovated. Three minutes' walk from Kingussie Station, at which all trains
stop. Hotel Porter attends all trains. Parties boarded per week or month. Inclusive
terms on application.

LARGE GARAGE.   **Oils and Petrol kept.**

LAWN TENNIS AND CROQUET GREEN IN HOTEL GROUNDS.   **BOWLING GREEN.**

GOLF COURSE (18 holes) 10 minutes' walk.   **FISHING, ETC.**

TELEGRAMS—   MR. AND MRS. W. WOLFENDEN,
" Wolfenden, Kingussie."   *Proprietors and Managers.*

. **KYLES OF BUTE.**

ROYAL HOTEL

AT AUCHENLOCHAN PIER, TIGHNABRUAICH.

Greatly Enlarged.   Pleasant Residence for Tourists and Families

COLF.   BILLIARDS.   LAWN TENNIS.   CARRIAGE HIRING.

Telegraphic Address : " ROYAL, TIGHNABRUAICH."
Telephone **5.**   **R. DUNCAN, Proprietor.**

LIMERICK.

CRUISE'S ROYAL HOTEL.

FIRST-CLASS FAMILY HOTEL.

Headquarters Irish Automobile, A.A., and Motor Union Clubs, American A.A. New Lounge. Ballroom capable of accommodating over 300 persons just added. Ladies' Drawing-Room, Billiard Room, Smoking Room, Excellent Cuisine, a Home from Home, Electric Light throughout. Free Garage. Hot, Cold, and Shower Baths.

Brochure and Tariff to be had on application to

JAMES FLYNN, Managing Proprietor.

LIVERPOOL.

Lancashire and Yorkshire Railway.

EXCHANGE STATION HOTEL.

(*Under the Management of the Company.*)

THE nearest First-Class Hotel to the Landing Stage. The Exchange Station is the terminus for the principal Express Trains from Scotland.

The Hotel is noted for the excellence of its cooking and comfortable accommodation.

Telegrams—"STATION HOTEL, LIVERPOOL." G. O'B. HAMILTON,
Telephone—2104 CENTRAL. *Manager.*

LIVERPOOL.

"THE SHAFTESBURY."
MOUNT PLEASANT.

A HIGH-CLASS TEMPERANCE HOUSE. Centrally situated. Quiet and homelike. About four minutes' walk from Lime Street and Central Stations, and adjoining Roscoe Gardens. Mount Pleasant Cars from Pier Head and Castle Street (*near Town Hall and Exchange Station*) stop at door of Hotel. Night Porter. Cab Fare from any Station, 1s. Good Stock Rooms.

Telegrams: "Shaftesbury Hotel, Liverpool." *Telephone :* 3882 Royal.

LIVERPOOL.

LAURENCE'S

COMMERCIAL & FAMILY TEMPERANCE HOTEL,
CLAYTON SQUARE

(*Within Three Minutes' Walk of Lime Street and Central Stations, and the Chief Objects of Interest in the Town*).

CONTAINS upwards of One Hundred Rooms, including Coffee Room, Private Sitting Rooms, Billiard and Smoke Rooms, Large and Well-Lighted Stock Rooms. **HEADQUARTERS CYCLISTS' TOURING CLUB.**

Telephone—Royal, No. 3729

BOOKS FOR SPORTSMEN.

AN ANGLER'S SEASON.

By WILLIAM EARL HODGSON. Containing 12 pages of Illustrations from photographs. Large crown 8vo, cloth. **Price 3/6 net.**
(*By Post, 3/10.*)

COARSE FISHING.

By H. T. SHERINGHAM. Large crown 8vo, cloth. Containing 42 Illustrations in the text. **Price 3/6 net.**
(*By Post, 3/10.*)

THE BOOK OF THE DRY FLY.

By GEORGE A. B. DEWAR. With contributions by HIS GRACE THE DUKE OF RUTLAND and Mr. J. E. BOOTH. Containing 8 full-page Illustrations in colour, 7 representing the most typical Dry-Fly Streams of England, and one a selection of natural Flies. *New Edition.* Large crown 8vo, cloth. **Price 7/6 net.**
(*By Post, 7/10.*)

DRY-FLY FISHING IN BORDER WATERS.

By F. FERNIE, A.M.I.C.E. With an Introduction by J. CUTHBERT HADDEN. Large crown 8vo, cloth, illustrated. **Price 2/6 net.**
(*By Post, 2/9.*)

HOW TO FISH.

By WILLIAM EARL HODGSON. Containing 8 full-page illustrations and 18 smaller Engravings in the text. Large crown 8vo, cloth. **Price 3/6 net.**
(*By Post, 3/11.*)

MINOR TACTICS OF THE CHALK STREAM: And Kindred Studies.

By G. E. M. SKUES (Seaforth and Soforth). *Second Edition.* Containing Frontispiece Plate of Flies in coloured facsimile. Royal 8vo, cloth. **Price 3/6 net.**
(*By Post, 3/11.*)

THE PRACTICAL ANGLER: Or, The Art of Trout Fishing more Particularly Applied to Clear Water.

By W. C. STEWART. *New Edition,* Containing an Introduction by WILLIAM EARL HODGSON, and including coloured facsimiles of the Flies used by Mr. Stewart. Large crown 8vo, cloth. **Price 3/6 net.**
(*By Post, 3/10.*)

SALMON FISHING.

By WILLIAM EARL HODGSON. Containing a facsimile in colours of a "Model Set of Flies" for Scotland, Ireland, England, and Wales, and 10 Illustrations from photographs. Large crown 8vo, cloth, gilt top. **Price 7/6 net.**
(*By Post, 7/11.*)

HOW TO DRESS SALMON FLIES.

By Dr. T. E. PRYCE-TANNATT. Containing 8 full-page Plates in colour of Salmon-Flies arranged by the author, and 101 line drawings in the text. Large crown 8vo, cloth, gilt top. **Price 7/6 net.**
(*By Post, 7/11.*)

LIFE-HISTORY AND HABITS OF THE SALMON, SEA-TROUT, TROUT, AND OTHER FRESH-WATER FISH.

By P. D. MALLOCH. *New Edition.* Containing 274 Illustrations from photographs. Crown 4to, cloth. **Price 10/6 net.**
(*By Post, 11/-.*)

SEA FISHING.

By C. O. MINCHIN. With 32 Illustrations in the text, mostly from original sketches by J. A. MINCHIN. Large crown 8vo, cloth. **Price 3/6 net.**
(*By Post, 3/10.*)

TROUT FISHING. — A Study of Natural Phenomena.

By WILLIAM EARL HODGSON. Containing a facsimile in colours of a "Model Book of Flies" for stream and lake, arranged according to the month in which the lures are appropriate. Large crown 8vo, cloth, gilt top. **Price 7/6 net.**
(*By Post, 7/11.*)

TROUT WATERS. — Management and Angling.

By WILSON H. ARMISTEAD. Large crown 8vo, cloth. **Price 3/6 net.**
(*By Post, 3/10.*)

THE ART OF WORM-FISHING. — A Practical Treatise on Clear-Water Worming.

By ALEXANDER MACKIE, M.A., author of *Aberdeenshire, Nature Knowledge in Modern Poetry,* etc. Large crown 8vo, cloth, Illustrated with Diagrams. **Price 1/6 net.**
(*By Post, 1/9.*)

GROUSE AND GROUSE MOORS.

By GEORGE MALCOLM and CAPTAIN AYMER MAXWELL. With 16 full-page Illustrations in colour by CHARLES WHYMPER, F.Z.S. Large crown 8vo, cloth, gilt top. **Price 7/6 net.**
(*By Post, 7/11.*)

PARTRIDGES AND PARTRIDGE MANORS.

By CAPTAIN AYMER MAXWELL. With 16 full-page Illustrations in colour by GEORGE RANKIN. Large crown 8vo, cloth, gilt top. **Price 7/6 net.**
(*By Post, 7/11.*)

PHEASANTS AND COVERT SHOOTING.

By CAPTAIN AYMER MAXWELL. Containing 16 full-page Illustrations in colour by GEORGE RANKIN. Large crown 8vo, cloth, gilt top. **Price 7/6 net.**
(*By Post, 7/11.*)

PUBLISHED BY A. & C. BLACK, LTD., 4, 5, & 6 SOHO SQUARE, LONDON, W.
And obtainable through all Booksellers.

C. C. & T. MOORE,

AUCTIONEERS,	VALUERS &
SURVEYORS,	ESTATE AGENTS.

7 LEADENHALL STREET, LONDON,

and 33 MILE END ROAD, E.

House Property Auctions [*held continuously for 79 years*] at the Mart on Thursdays. Special Attention to the Management of Houses and Estates, and letting City Offices and Business Property.

WHITE HALL
RESIDENTIAL HOTELS
(close to the British Museum)
RUSSELL SQUARE, W.C.

9, 10 & 11 BLOOMSBURY SQUARE
Telegraph: "TASTEFUL, London."
Telephone: 9\11 Museum.

TERMS—From 8s. per day, or 2½ Guineas per week, including Bedroom, Table d'hote Breakfast, Tea, Dinner, Lights, and Attendance.

18, 19 & 20 MONTAGUE STREET
Telegraph: "RIPELY, London."
Telephone: 5707 Central.

70, 71 & 72 GUILFORD STREET
Telegraph: "LUGGAGE, London."
Telephone: 9909 Central.

4 & 5 MONTAGUE STREET
Telegraph: "WHITENTIAL, London."
Telephone: 11442 Central.

15 & 16 BEDFORD PLACE
Telegraph: "QUIVERED, London."
Telephone: 8247 Central.

22 MONTAGUE STREET
Telegraph: "SIGNOR, London."
Telephone: 7117 Central.

From 7s. per day or 2 Guineas per week.

13 WOBURN PLACE
Telegraph: "QUEENHOOD, London."
Telephone: 12491 Central.

23 & 22 CORAM STREET
Telegraph: "WAYFARING, London."
Telephone: 13880 Central.

From 6s. per day or 38s. 6d. per week.

LOSSIEMOUTH.

STOTFIELD HOTEL.

A PERFECT GOLFER'S RETREAT.

TWO SPLENDID GOLF COURSES (9 AND 18 HOLES).

EXCELLENT BATHING BEACH. MODERATE TERMS.

MAGNIFICENT NEW LOUNGE.   **ELECTRIC LIGHT.**

MOTOR CAR ACCOMMODATION. PETROL, Etc., Etc.

Tariff on application to **WILLIAM CHRISTIE,** *Proprietor.*

LOUGH SWILLY, CO. DONEGAL.

PORTSALON HOTEL.

THIS excellent Hotel, which affords first-class accommodation and every comfort to Families, Golfers, and other Tourists, is magnificently situated, with southern aspect, and commands sea and mountain views of matchless beauty. The Golf Links (18 holes) are most sporting and picturesque. Good lake and sea fishing. Boating, Bathing, Tennis, Croquet, Billiards, Garage, Dark Room for Photography. etc. Route *via* Strabane and Letterkenny, thence (during summer months) by Hotel Motor. Telegrams—" Hotel, Portsalon."

Illustrated Brochure on application to MANAGER.

LYDFORD.

MANOR HOTEL.

FIVE minutes from South-Western and Great Western Stations. Sheltered situation on fringe of Dartmoor. 26 Bedrooms. Comfortably furnished. First-class Coffee and Drawing Rooms. The extensive private grounds of 50 acres include the beautiful wooded valley and gorge of River Lyd, and celebrated Lydford Waterfall. Tennis Lawn. Fishing, Rough Shooting. Hotel lighted throughout by Gas. Under personal management of Proprietress, MRS. MATHEWS. Newly built Stables. Garage. Excellent Cuisine.   **Terms moderate, on application.**

Telegrams: HOLMAN.

LYNTON.

VALLEY OF ROCKS HOTEL.

Largest and Principal.

SITUATED IN OWN GROUNDS.

600 *Feet above and facing Sea.*

Passenger Lift.

Radiator Heating.

Write for New Illustrated Tariff.

Motor Garage.

Resident Proprietor.

Telephone: No. 49.

LYNTON.
IMPERIAL HOTEL.
Beautifully Situated.
Facing Sea.
Luxurious Lounge newly added.
Electric Light throughout.
Moderate Terms.
Motor Garage.

Telephone: No. 50 LYNTON.

Telegrams: "IMPERIAL,"
LYNTON.

MALVERN.
THE ABBEY HOTEL.
IN EXCELLENT SITUATION.
MOST COMFORTABLE FAMILY HOTEL.
New and Commodious Coffee and Smoking Rooms have been opened, and Suites of Rooms with Private Bath added.

Perfect Sanitary Arrangements. *Electric Light throughout.*
Telephone—**No. 183.** **GARAGE.** *For Tariff apply Manager.*

MALVERN.
THE FOLEY ARMS HOTEL.
(PATRONISED BY THE ROYAL FAMILY.)

"THE first time we visited Malvern, when shown into an upper chamber in the 'FOLEY ARMS,' we were literally taken aback. We can hardly say more than that the prospect struck us as far finer than from the terrace over the Thames at Richmond, etc., etc."—*Extract from article in* "*Blackwood,*" *August 1884.*

Coffee Room and Drawing Room for Ladies and Gentlemen. Table d'Hôte at Separate Tables. Electric Light. Perfect Sanitary arrangements.
Telephone—No. 197 Malvern. MISS YOUNGER, *Proprietress.*

MALVERN.
HARDWICKE PRIVATE HOTEL.
Enjoys the highest reputation. Bathrooms. Electric Light throughout the building. :: All Modern Conveniences.
NEAREST HOTEL TO THE COLLEGE AND GOLF LINKS.
TELEGRAMS AND TELEPHONE—**246** MALVERN. H. WILSON, *Proprietor.*

A Guide to the places of Historic Interest, Natural Beauty, or Literary Association.
WHAT TO SEE IN ENGLAND.
BY GORDON HOME.

New Edition, revised and rearranged, containing 155 Page Illustrations. Crown 8vo, cloth.
Price 3/6 net. (By Post 3/10.)
PUBLISHED BY A. & C. BLACK, LTD., 4, 5, & 6 SOHO SQUARE, LONDON, W.
And obtainable through any Bookseller.

MULLION, CORNWALL.

POLDHU HOTEL.

FIRST Class, Largest in District, Lounge, Electric Light throughout, close to Sea, commands magnificent views of Mounts Bay with its grand Cliff Scenery. Good Beach. Excellent Bathing. Lock-up Garage.

Adjoining splendid Golf Links, 18 Holes.

Tariff Moderate.   *Apply* MANAGER.

MULLION, SOUTH CORNWALL.

POLURRIAN HOTEL.

FIRST CLASS.   Stands in its own grounds of 4 acres ; replete in all modern appointments ; Large Lounge ; Electric Light ; Facing Sea ; Good Boating, Fishing, and Bathing ; Excellent Sands ; near Splendid Golf Links (18 holes) ; Visitors driven free to same at stated times ; Garage.   Station, Helston.   Terms moderate.

Apply MANAGER.

NAIRN.

THE WAVERLEY HOTEL.

THE MOST COMFORTABLE AND CENTRAL HOTEL IN TOWN, being nearest to Station and Post Office, and within a few minutes' walk of Golf Courses and Beach.

Recommended as one of the Best Temperance Hotels in Scotland.

There are 26 Well-Lighted Bedrooms, Bathrooms, Large Dining Room, "Separate Tables," Drawing, Commercial and Smoke Rooms.

Breakfast and Teas, 1s. to 2s. Bedroom and Attendance from 2s. 6d. Weekly Terms £2:2s.   From 7s. per Day.

Headquarters C.T.C. and A.C.U.

Garage close to Hotel.   *Boots attends all Trains.*

Telephone No. 77.   **J. G. CHISHOLM.**

NEWCASTLE, CO. DOWN.

SLIEVE DONARD HOTEL,

FINEST HOTEL IN IRELAND.

OWNED AND MANAGED BY BELFAST AND COUNTY DOWN RAILWAY CO.

STANDS IN ITS OWN GROUNDS OF 12 ACRES.   Faces Sea and Mourne Mountains ; Royal County Down Golf Links (18 holes) immediately adjoining.   Separate course for ladies.   Spacious Reception Rooms and Lounge; 120 Bedrooms.   Electric Light in all Rooms ; Passenger Lift ; Hall and Corridors Heated ; Hot and Cold Sea and Fresh Water Baths.   Croquet and Lawn Tennis Courts.

Tariff on application to J. W. MANNING, *Manager.*

Telegrams : "SLIEVE, NEWCASTLE, DOWN."   *Telephone :* 6.

NEWCASTLE-ON-TYNE.

THE TYNE TEMPERANCE HOTEL,

HOOD STREET, NEAR TO MONUMENT.

VISITORS will find every comfort combined with moderate charges. Coffee Drawing, Commercial, Smoke and Billiard Rooms. Electric Light throughout Good Stock Rooms. National Telephone, 2144 Central. Telegrams, "Tyne Hotel."

NEWQUAY.

HOTEL EDGCUMBE.

BEAUTIFULLY situated, with magnificent and uninterrupted view of the Atlantic Ocean and surrounding country. Overlooking bathing beaches.

RECREATION ROOM.　　　LOCK-UP GARAGES.

TELEPHONE 27.　　　　**Apply Manageress.**

NEWQUAY.

"PENOLVER," PRIVATE HOTEL.
En Pension.

Uninterrupted Sea View. Path to Beaches from House. Easy access to Golf Links. 3 minutes from Railway Station. Electric Light. Best Position. Highly Recommended. Tariff, etc., on application.

Telegrams—"Littlejohn, Newquay."　Jno. LITTLEJOHN (Late of) Exeter.), *Proprietor.*

MARINE HOTEL
ESPLANADE, OBAN.

1 min. Pier, 3 mins. Station.
The Largest and Leading Temperance Hotel. Upwards of 100 Rooms.
Lounge overlooking Bay.

Inclusive Terms throughout the Season.

This High-Class unlicensed Hotel is one of the most popular houses in Scotland, and is well known for its excellent plain cooking and very moderate tariff.

Booklet Sent.

FRANK WALTON, *Proprietor.*

OBAN.

GREAT WESTERN HOTEL,

LARGEST AND LEADING HOTEL IN THE WEST HIGHLANDS.

Official Hotel S.A.C. ; A.A. ; and Touring Club of America.

Beautifully situated on Esplanade. Electric Light. Elevator. Charges moderate. Special inclusive rates prior to 15th July and after 15th September. Illustrated Tariff Booklet post free. Motor-'Bus meets Trains and Steamers and conveys Visitors to Hotel Free of Charge. Garage. Petrol.

ALEX. McGREGOR, *Resident Proprietor.*

Telegraphic Address—"WESTERN OBAN." 'Phone—No. 4 OBAN.

OBAN.

KING'S ARMS HOTEL.

FIRST-CLASS FAMILY AND TOURIST HOTEL.

ON the Promenade, midway between Railway Station and Pier. Facing the Bay. Magnificent Sea View. A.A. & M.U. Headquarters. Coupons accepted. Rebuilt and enlarged. Boarding. Will be found replete. Near Golf Course (18 holes). Porters await arrival of all trains and steamers. **J. M. MacTAVISH, Proprietor and Manager.**

OBAN.

PALACE
TEMPERANCE HOTEL,
GEORGE STREET, OBAN.

Every Home Comfort.
Boots waits Train and Steamer.

DREW'S HOTELS.

The "Wynnstay," Oswestry. 30 Rooms.

Appointed R.A.C. and Motor Union. Tel. No. 38 Oswestry.

The "Queen's," Ilfracombe. 30 Rooms.

B. and B., 5s. Tel. No. 66 Ilfracombe.

The "Imperial," Ilfracombe. 100 Rooms.

B. and B., 5s. Tel. No. 22 Ilfracombe.

The "Lamb," Cheltenham. 24 Rooms.

B. and B., 5s. Tel. No. 931 Cheltenham.

Every Comfort and Accommodation for Motorists. Moderate Charges.
Electric Light in All. **GOOD GARAGES.**

OXFORD.

RANDOLPH HOTEL,

BEAUMONT STREET,

IN THE CENTRE OF THE CITY.

THE modern Hotel of Oxford, close to the Colleges, Publi Buildings, and opposite Martyrs' Memorial. Replete wit every comfort and convenience.

Handsome Suites of Rooms ; Lounge, Drawing, Smoking, and Billiard Rooms.

NEW GARAGE. AN AMERICAN ELEVATOR. CHARGES MODERATE
A Night Porter in Attendance.
ELECTRIC LIGHT THROUGHOUT.

Address—THE MANAGER.

OXFORD.

THE MITRE HOTEL,

SITUATED in the centre of the finest Street in Europe, is one of tl most ECONOMICAL First-Class Hotels in the Kingdom. Dinin Drawing, Reading, and Smoking Rooms. Lounge and Spacious Billiaı Room. Electric Light. Night Porter.

'Phone 335. Telegrams: "MITRE, OXFORD.' **Apply Miss THORNE,** *Manageress.*

OXFORD.

OXENFORD HALL, 13 to 17 MAGDALEN S
PRIVATE AND RESIDENTIAL HOTEL.
Terms Moderate. In the Centre of City. Near Colleges, and opposite Martyrs' Memorial. Telephone 74 MISS WATSO

PLYMOUTH.

DUKE OF CORNWALL HOTEL.

The leading and largest Hotel, centrally situated near Railway Station and Sea Front.   Recognised Hotel for Ocean Passengers.

GARAGE.   ELECTRIC LIGHT AND LIFT.

HOTEL OMNIBUS MEETS ALL TRAINS.

Telegrams: "DUKOTEL."   "R.A.C." and "A.A."

PORTHCAWL.

ESPLANADE HOTEL.

First-class Residential.

100 Rooms.

R.A.C.   **A.A. and M.U.**
District Hotel.   **Registered Hotel.**

Best Situation.
First-class Cuisine.

Moderate Inclusive Terms according t
Room and Season.

Nearest Licensed Hotel to the
ROYAL PORTHCAWL GOLF LINKS.

*Special discount to Officers (convalescent)
invalided from the Front.*

PORTRUSH, CO. ANTRIM.

NORTHERN COUNTIES HOTEL.

(Under the Management of the Midland Railway Company.)

FINEST GOLF LINKS IN IRELAND.

SPLENDID SUITES OF SEA AND FRESH WATER BATHS.

Electric Light throughout.   **Garage for 20 Motors**

Lounge Hall.   *Magnificent Ballroom.*

Telegrams—"MIDOTEL, PORTRUSH." Telephone No. 14.

Full particulars on application to
F. AUDINWOOD, *Manager, Northern Counties Committee's Hotels, etc*

PORTSMOUTH.

SPEEDWELL

(TEMPERANCE)

FAMILY AND COMMERCIAL HOTEL, OPPOSITE TOWN STATION.

(Book for Portsmouth Town.)

Every accommodation for Commercial and Private Visitors.
NIGHT BOOTS.   **RESTAURANT.**

ALFRED GRIGSBY, *Proprietor.*

ROSS-ON-WYE.

ROYAL HOTEL.

On an eminence overlooking River.

ROSS IS THE GATE OF THE WYE (THE RHINE OF ENGLAND).

THE only Hotel in the Town with a Garden, Pleasure Grounds, and an uninterrupted view of the River. Every Comfort. Moderate Charges. Electric Light. Posting. Golf. Fishing. Motor Garage and I. P. Petrol.   Tel. : 40.

ST. FILLANS, LOCH EARN—PERTHSHIRE.

DRUMMOND ARMS HOTEL.

FIRST-CLASS FAMILY AND TOURIST HOTEL.

SPLENDIDLY SITUATED AT THE FOOT OF LOCH EARN.

GOLF. FISHING. BOATING. POSTING. GARAGE.

TERMS MODERATE.

TELEGRAMS—Hotel, St. Fillans.   R. A. CAMPBELL, *Proprietor.*

In connection with Station Hotel, Oban.

ST. IVES (CORNWALL).

TREVESSA

PRIVATE AND RESIDENTIAL HOTEL.

MODERATE TERMS EN PENSION.

Unrivalled Position overlooking the Bay.
Three Minutes from Station and Beach.   Near Golf Links.

SPECIAL WINTER TERMS.

ALSO FURNISHED HOUSE.

Telephone 43.   MISS V. NEWTON.

SARK, CHANNEL ISLANDS.

HÔTEL BEL-AIR.

On the most bracing spot in the Island.   A first-class country hotel.

THE largest and only Hotel on the island with a sea view. Possesses excellent sleeping accommodation; large Public, Drawing, Smoking, and Dining Rooms (separate tables).

Good Fishing and Bathing; Croquet and Tennis.   Terms moderate.

N.B.—The Sark steamer leaves Guernsey at 10 A.M. daily (Saturdays at 11 A.M.) during the summer months. Passage about one hour. Carriages and Porter from the Hotel meet the Steamer.

BLACK'S BRITISH POST CARDS.

Beautiful Reproductions in Colour from Pictures by well-known Artists.

Series 2, 3, and 4.   THE CHANNEL ISLANDS.   Three packets of six cards each.   *Price 6d. per packet.*

PUBLISHED BY A. & C. BLACK, LTD., 4, 5, & 6 SOHO SQUARE, LONDON, W.

WORKINGTON.

CENTRAL HOTEL.

(Adjoining Central Railway Station.)

EXTENSIVE ALTERATIONS COMPLETED. ONE OF THE FINEST AND MOST LUXURIOUS DINING-HALLS IN THE NORTH.

Hotel appointed by the Automobile Association and Motor Union.

Good Stock Rooms.   **Garage.**

Posting in all its Branches.   'Bus meets all Trains.

Telephone 250.   J. KERLY, *Proprietor.*

GREAT YARMOUTH.

The Leading Family Hotels:—

THE QUEEN'S, Tel. No. 28.

**Fine New Lounge. 125 Rooms. Electric Light.
New Motor Garage. R.A.C. & A.A. Hotel.**

THE ROYAL, Tel. No. 26.

**Select Position. Winter Gardens and Lounge.
R.A.C. & A.A. Hotel. 100 Rooms. Electric Light.**

THESE two first-class Family Hotels each occupy a commanding position on the Marine Parade, with magnificent Sea Views, and opposite the Beach Gardens.

ILLUSTRATED TARIFFS POST FREE.

W. NIGHTINGALE, *Proprietor.*

FURNESS RAILWAY.

(CONISTON FROM BEACON CRAGS.)

20 Rail, Coach, and Steam Yacht
TOURS THROUGH LAKELAND

EVERY WEEK-DAY

From July 12th to September 30th.

The following Tours embrace the chief places of interest in the Lake District.

No. 1.—**Outer Circular Tour,** embracing Windermere Lake, Furness Abbey, and Coniston.

No. 2.—**Inner Circular Tour,** embracing Furness Abbey, Coniston Lake, and Crake Valley.

No. 4.—**Middle Circular Tour,** embracing Windermere Lake, the Crake Valley, and Coniston Lake.

No. 5.—**Red Bank and Grasmere Tour,** *via* Ambleside and Skelwith Force.

No. 10.—**Round the Langdales and Dungeon Ghyll Tour,** *via* Ambleside, Colwith Force, Grasmere, and Rydal.

No. 13.—**Five Lakes Circular Tour,** viz.—**Windermere, Rydal, Grasmere, Thirlmere, and Derwentwater.**

No. 14.—**Wastwater Tour,** *via* Seascale, and Gosforth. Churchyard Cross, A.D. 680.

No. 15.—**Six Lakes Circular Tour,** viz.—**Windermere, Rydal, Grasmere, Thirlmere, Derwentwater, and Ullswater.**

No. 16.—**Duddon Valley Tour,** *via* Broughton-in-Furness, Ulpha, and Seathwaite.

No. 20.—**George Romney's Home (1742 to 1755), Walney Bridge and Island, and Furness Abbey Tour,** *via* Sowerby Wood.

For further particulars see the Company's Illustrated Tours Programme, to be had gratis at all Furness Railway Stations; from Mr. A. A. Haynes, Superintendent of the Line, Barrow-in-Furness; and at the Offices of Messrs. Thos. Cook & Son; also at the principal Bookstalls.

BLACKPOOL AND THE LAKES
In connection with the Company's Paddle Steamers 'LADY EVELYN' & 'LADY MOYRA.'

Every Week-day from July 12th to September 30th.
THE OUTER CIRCULAR TOUR

(This Combination provides an ideal Day's Picnic Tour), by *Sea, Rail, Lake,* and *Coach,* embracing **Furness Abbey, Windermere Lake** and **Coniston.**

ALFRED ASLETT,

BARROW-IN-FURNESS, *April* 1915.   *Secretary and General Manager.*

THE BEST WAY TO THE THEATRES

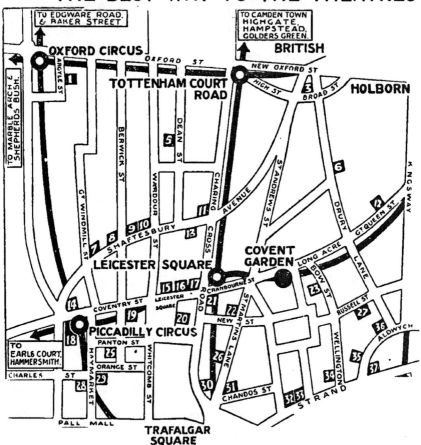

KEY TO THEATRE PLAN.

32 Adelphi	27 Drury Lane	6 Middlesex Music Hall	St. James's
36 Aldwych	26 Duke of York's	22 New	(*Dover St. and S*
20 Alhambra	15 Empire | 30 Garrick	5 New Royalty	*James's Park Stn*
8 Apollo	37 Gaiety | 9 Globe	2 Oxford Music Hall	Scala (*Goodge St*
31 Coliseum	29 Haymarket	11 Palace	*S. W.*)
25 Comedy	17 Hippodrome	1 Palladium	13 Shaftesbur
Coronet (*Notting*	28 His Majesty's	14 Pavilion	35 Strand
Hill Gate.) [S. W.]	4 Holborn Empire	38 Playhouse	39 The Little
Court (*Sloane Sq.,*	12 Kingsway	19 Prince of Wales	33 Vaudeville
23 Covent Garden	24 London Opera House	3 Princes	Victoria Palac
18 Criterion	34 Lyceum	Queen's	

DEVONSHIRE.

Lynton & Barnstaple Railway

This Narrow-gauge Picturesque Line affords connection at BARNSTAPLE (Town Station) with the Main Line Trains of the London and South-Western Railway Company, and gives

|| THE BEST AND QUICKEST ROUTE TO LYNTON AND LYNMOUTH FROM ALL PARTS ||

For Time Tables, etc., apply—
"GENERAL MANAGER," L. & B. RAILWAY, BARNSTAPLE.

TO ANGLERS.

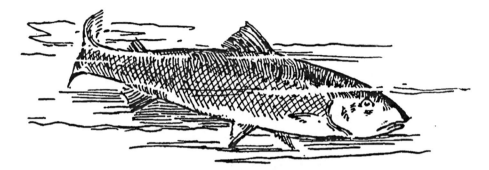

W. J. CUMMINS, Ltd.

Will send their Magnificent Catalogue and Angler's Guide FREE to any Address.

This interesting book has over 200 pages, many hundreds of Illustrations, and Original Articles on Fly, Worm, and Minnow Fishing for Trout, Salmon Fishing, Hints to Anglers visiting Norway, Canada, New Zealand, &c.

This publication has been highly praised and recommended by all the principal Sporting Papers.

FISHINGS TO LET.

Information gladly given regarding Fishing Outfits for any part of the World.

Write for particulars of Cummins' "Angler's Information Bureau."

Special Salmon and Trout Flies for Ireland, including Lough Conn, Connemara District, Killarney, the Rosses Fishery, &c. Selected List of over Seventy Patterns for the Trout Rivers of the United Kingdom. Special Patterns for the Scotch Lochs. Special Flies and Tackle for Norway.

W. J. CUMMINS, LTD.

North of England Rod Works, Bishop Auckland.

ESTABLISHED 1857.

Has no peer for safety

The "Safety Tread" Tyre

THE B.F. GOODRICH CO., LTD.

117 GOLDEN LANE, LONDON, E.C.

See their Illustrated Catalogue for proof.

WEST OF SCOTLAND
SANITARY ASSOCIATION

SANITARY SURVEYS AND REPORTS.

This Association employs a permanent staff of experienced Engineers, and furnishes reports on Sewage Disposal, Drainage, Sanitary Appliances, Water Supplies in town or country, and hot water and heating arrangements. Plans are prepared, estimates obtained, and the whole work supervised during its progress. The Association is not formed for purposes of profit. Further particulars may be had on application to the Secretary.

President.
Sir JAMES BELL, Bart., Ex-Lord Provost of Glasgow.

Vice-Presidents.
Sir THOS. GLEN COATS, Bart., Paisley.
Sir MATTHEW ARTHUR, Bart., Fullarton, Troon.

Secretary and Treasurer.
W. R. M. CHURCH, C.A., 104 WEST GEORGE STREET, GLASGOW
Telegraphic Address—"CHURCH," GLASGOW.   Telephone—3405 DOUGLAS

"Healthy Houses."
SANITARY PROTECTION ASSOCIATION.
ESTABLISHED 1878.
Head Office: No. 5 ALVA STREET, EDINBURGH.
Telegraphic Address—"*HEALTH, EDINBURGH.*"   *Telephone No.*—662 Central.

The Association employs a permanent staff of experienced Engineers, and is thus able to furnish REPORTS, at the shortest notice, on the SEWAGE DISPOSAL DRAINAGE, SANITARY APPLIANCES, and WATER SUPPLY of HOUSES in TOWN or COUNTRY, or to prepare plans, obtain estimates, and supervise the execution of any such new work required. The Rates of Subscription and any other information may be obtained from the Secretary, R. BLACKADDER, Esq.

Tomato Catsup

Ask for it at
your Hotel
WHEN TAKING YOUR HOLI
DAY IT WILL ADD TO YOUR
ENJOYMENT IF YOU HAV
G.D. CATSUP WIT
YOUR FISH OR MEAT.

3d., 6d., 9d. and 1s. per Bottle.
SIMPLY ASK YOUR GROCER FOR A BOTTLE OF
G.D. TOMATO CATSUP.

SUN FIRE OFFICE

(206th YEAR).

Copied from Policy dated 1726.

HEAD OFFICE:

63 THREADNEEDLE

STREET, E.C.

FOUNDED 1710

THE OLDEST

INSURANCE

OFFICE IN THE

WORLD.

BRANCHES.

London, 60 Charing Cross.
,, 332 Oxford Street.
,, 40 Chancery Lane.
,, 42 Mincing Lane.
Birmingham, 10 Bennett's Hill.
Potteries (Sub-Branch), 10 Pall Mall, Hanley.
Brighton, 3 Prince's Place, North Street.
Bristol, Clare Street.
Cardiff, 13 Windsor Place.
Swansea (Sub-Branch), 7 & 8 Oxford Street.
Hull, Lowgate.
Ipswich, Sun Buildings.
Leeds, 15 Park Row.
Sub-Branches:—
Bradford, Market Street.
Halifax, 15 Commercial Street.

Leeds (Sub-Branches—contd.)—
Huddersfield, St. George's Square.
Sheffield, 62 & 64 Fargate.
Liverpool, 6 Chapel Street.
Manchester, 84 King Street.
Blackburn (Sub-Branch), Richmond Ter.
Newcastle-on-Tyne, Collingwood Street.
Carlisle (Sub-Branch), 2 Lowther Street.
Nottingham, 19 Low Pavement.
Plymouth, 59 Bedford Street.
Reading, 33 Blagrave Street.
Southampton, High Street.
Edinburgh, 40 Princes Street.
Aberdeen (Sub-Branch), 46A Union St.
Dundee (Sub-Branch), 33 Albert Square.
Glasgow, 42 Renfield Street.
Dublin, 9 College Green.
Belfast (Sub-Branch), 38 Rosemary St.

Insurances effected against the following Risks:—

FIRE.

RESULTANT LOSS OF RENT AND PROFITS.
EMPLOYERS' LIABILITY and WORKMEN'S COMPENSATION,
including ACCIDENTS TO DOMESTIC SERVANTS.
PERSONAL ACCIDENT.   SICKNESS and DISEASE.
FIDELITY GUARANTEE.   BURGLARY.   PLATE GLASS.

MODERATE RATES.   PROMPT SETTLEMENTS.
LOSSES BY LIGHTNING ADMITTED UNDER FIRE POLICIES.
APPLICATIONS FOR AGENCIES INVITED.

GEO. E. MEAD, *Manager and Secretary.*

BLACK'S
ANNUALS & BOOKS OF REFERENCE

WHO'S WHO, 1915.

Large post 8vo, cloth.   **Price 15s. net.**   (By post 15s. 6d.)
Or bound in full red leather, with rounded corners and gilt edges.
         Price 20s. net.   (By post 20s. 6d.)
This year's issue contains over 25,000 biographies.

WHO'S WHO YEAR BOOK, 1914-15.

Containing Tables complementary to the information given in WHO'S
   WHO.   **Price 1s. net.**   (By post 1s. 3d.)

ENGLISHWOMAN'S YEAR-BOOK AND DIRECTORY, 1915.

Edited by **G. E. Mitton.**
Thirty-fourth Year of Issue. Crown 8vo, cloth.
         Price 2s. 6d. net.   (By post 2s. 10d.)

THE WRITERS' AND ARTISTS' YEAR=BOOK, 1915.

A Directory for Writers, Artists, and Photographers.
Tenth Year of New Issue. Crown 8vo, cloth.
         Price 1s. net.   (By post 1s. 3d.)

BLACK'S MEDICAL DICTIONARY.

By **J. D. Comrie, M.A., B.Sc., M.D., F.R.C.P.E.**
Fifth Edition, completing 30,000 copies. Containing 425 illustrations
   12 being full-page in colour.
Demy 8vo, cloth.   **Price 7s. 6d. net.**   (By post 8s.)

BOOKS THAT COUNT.
A DICTIONARY OF STANDARD BOOKS.

Edited by **W. Forbes Gray.**
Crown 8vo, cloth.   **Price 5s. net.**   (By post 5s. 4d.)

It gives details of about 5500 works, in all departments of literature (except in fiction), arranged in sections and fully indexed, thus facilitating ready reference.

CAREERS FOR OUR SONS.

A Practical Handbook to the Professions and Commercial Life.
Edited by **George H. Williams, M.A. (Oxon.).**
Fourth Edition, revised throughout and enlarged.
Crown 8vo, cloth.   **Price 5s. net.**   (By post 5s. 4d.)

PUBLISHED BY A. & C. BLACK, LTD., 4, 5, & 6 SOHO SQUARE, LONDON, W.
And obtainable of all Booksellers.

FIRE

LIFE

MARINE

ACCIDENT

Capital fully Subscribed	£2,950,000
Capital Paid up	£295,000
Life Funds	£5,650,889
Special Trust Funds:—	
"West of England"	538,256
"Hand in Hand".	3,732,116
"Union Life Fund"	4,044,087
Other Assets	10,936,904
Total, 31st December 1913 . .	£24,902,252
Total Annual Income exceeds	£8,500,000

The following classes of Insurance effected :—

FIRE, LIFE and ANNUITIES, MARINE, LEASEHOLD REDEMPTION and SINKING FUND.

ACCIDENT, including Personal Accident, Third Party, Burglary, Plate Glass, Fidelity Guarantee, Employers' Liability, Workmen's Compensation, and Servants' Insurance.

The Company will act as TRUSTEES and EXECUTORS under Wills.

PROSPECTUSES and all information needful for effecting Assurances may be obtained at any of the Company's Offices or Agencies throughout the world.

EDINBURGH BRANCH . . 10 North St. David Street.

LOCAL BOARD.

GEO. BENNET CLARK, Esq., W.S., Edin.   JAMES M. GRAY, Esq., Solicitor, Dundee.
ISAAC CONNELL, Esq., S.S.C., Edin.   ALEXANDER LAWSON, Esq., of Burnturk,
ROBT. F. DUDGEON, Esq., of Cargen,   Kettle, Fife.
Dumfries.   JOHN C. SCOTT, Esq., of Synton, Hawick.
GRAHAM G. WATSON, Esq., W.S., Edinburgh.

W. P. WILSON BRODIE, C.A., *District Manager*.

5

Banish dust, dirt and germs from floors, furniture and linoleum, by using

RONUK

—The Sanitary Polish for the Home.

Sold everywhere.   In tins, 3d., 6d., 1s., & 2s.

CPSIA information can be obtained
at www.ICGtesting.com
Printed in the USA
LVOW10s0620260617
539372LV00013B/116/P

9 781334 243547